Bullets

Growing Up in the Crossfire

Every experience is another Chapter

Kat Hibbard

BridgewayBooks

Bullets: Growing Up in the Crossfire
Published by Bridgeway Books
P.O. Box 80107
Austin, TX 78758

For more information about our books, please write to us, call
512.478.2028, or visit our website at www.bridgewaybooks.net.

Library of Congress Control Number: 2006939938

ISBN-13: 978-1-933538-82-2
ISBN-10: 1-933538-82-1

The essays in this book detail true-life experiences. Many of the ac-
counts were recalled for the first time since their happening. The
process of writing this book resurfaced many more than I was aware
of during the planning process. I took these strange but true stories
and recorded them to the best of my knowledge, memory, and feelings. The result is my translation, complete with comparisons, com-
mentary, and reflections.

10 9 8 7 6 5 4 3 2 1

In memory of:
Pastor David Owens,
who taught me to see beyond
what is in front of me
and to reach for
what is out of my grasp.

Acknowledgments

My undying gratitude goes out to the BookPros, Bridgeway, and Phenix and Phenix teams. From our preliminary conversations and throughout the publishing process, each team member approached my project and my concerns with professionalism, interest, enthusiasm, and courtesy. Publishing a first book is a big and scary step for an author, and this unique and dedicated group of people guided me through it with expert hands.

If not for my sister Joanne and her husband, Jim, I would not have signed the publishing contract. Through emotional and financial support, they gave me the strength and confidence to keep this project alive.

To Tom and Suzy Van Cleave for their constant inspiration and for taking me seriously enough to write the check.

Prayers of thanks to Pastor Stephanie Perdew and the First Congregational Church of Wilmette for keeping me going when I ran out of energy and hope.

To my friends, colleagues, and mentors; I would not have finished this memoir without your constant words of encouragement.

In a completely adult-driven move, my children told me to take the risk and publish the book. Bailey and Logan give me the power to make anything happen. They have healed my fractured spirit and show me every day what it means to be alive and vital.

Thanks to Sue Poedtke at Bosch Marketing for getting the book into alternative venues and for her creativity put forth on my behalf.

And finally, to my mom who taught me to laugh at adversity and to love under the worst of circumstances. Her spirit is stronger than she will ever know. She can be heard saying that she doesn't know how she raised such strong, compassionate, and successful daughters. She should take a look in the mirror and understand that strength does not fall from the sky; it comes from a mother's love.

Introduction

A bullet is a fired projectile; it pierces, damages, and completely alters the target it has come in contact with. *Bullets* is written in essay form and relays the tragic details of my life with sarcasm, satire, wit, and painful honesty. A host of characters (all very real but addressed with fictional names), dance in and out of *Bullets,* but all leave an indelible memory. In an attempt to soften my startling reality, my parents are called only by pronouns; other key players are identified by nicknames descriptive of their roles in this adventure.

When I began to write this tale, I wasn't sure of the purpose. I have always written as a way for me to discover what I am really thinking. As the details of my childhood experiences reveal themselves to you, it will become apparent that I was taught to lock away my feelings and thoughts. It is a typical human response to shut down emotionally in order to shield our spirits from great trauma and pain. This response was augmented by a lesson I learned early in life from my father: you are supposed to just shut up and take it. I was trained to never cry out for help and to never protest his insane behavior. He saw it as a loss of control. This made the effects of His disease, manic depression, even more volatile.

And so, writing later in my life was a way to reclaim my feelings—a way to start the slow thaw out of the numbness I've felt most of my life. It is an extremely cathartic process. I type and watch the feelings flow onto the screen. I usually wait for at least one day before revisiting what has come out. I am often shocked by what is there—so personal, so relevant, and yet so new to my conscious self. Often while I am writing the details, I am also reliving them for the first time since the incident. This, I believe, is the element that makes the material so powerful and thought-provoking.

There is no way for someone to magically recover from the kinds of horrors that you are about to read. My recovery is still taking place and is the result of an incredible therapist, who found the keys to the Black Room where all of the feelings from my past were locked. As I parent my own children, I am also able to reclaim a little of the childhood that was taken away from me. Another part of the healing process is this book. I am able to articulate what happened to me and put each event in a place that makes sense. I feel like I am building a puzzle. Each essay takes a piece of a broken spirit and fits it with more pieces to finally rebuild the whole person. This is so powerful that I can't contain it within me, and now I am inspired to give the story to you.

Induced Labor

She was seven and a half months pregnant. He sat matter-of-factly molding soap into bullets. It was October in the year 1964. This surprise pregnancy had forced Them to the alter before They were ready. They were so young: She eighteen, He twenty-five. Neither had a clue how to care for Themselves, and soon a fragile soul would be placed in Their care.

She came from a family with three children. She was the middle. Her mom was kind, nurturing, and practiced the avoidance of conflict. Her dad was an overbearing, self-centered, hardened man, broken by his own family strife and war.

She had been pregnant before, at age fifteen. She'd been alone and hadn't known where to turn: to Her mom, who would want to avoid the situation, or Her dad, who would only demoralize Her further. She hid the pregnancy for nine months and then silently went into the basement and gave birth. In order not to create a family scandal, the child was whisked away and given up for adoption. A brief hospital stay was explained away as appendicitis.

So She sat, Her belly heavy and Her heart burdened with memories of the time before. Would this child also suffer the consequences of Her naïve carelessness? And what of this man, who Himself had endured the perils of reckless childbearing?

His own spirit had been broken before it was formed. His father had served as the family's dictator, His sister the caretaker, and His mother as the financial and domestic support.

He also carried a sickness that had been passed down without mention—alcoholism, fueled by manic depression. The fire that had burned others before Him, He carried. So far, He had kept it clasped in His palms where no one could see. This ugliness, however, was about to be released. It is possible that it was being used to mold those bullets out of soap. This is not the kind of thing that people usually sit and do just to kill time. But who's to say what a madman's objectives are?

Yes, my father was a madman. I don't think He had a real idea what havoc He was about to inflict on that helpless, unborn child. His whims would always take priority. So, on that day, October 11, 1964, He decided to take His bullet-making one step further.

There She sat, sewing curtains and bedding for the new baby, when He said, "Don't move."

He told Her They was going to play a little game of Russian roulette.

Pop!

He pulled the trigger and nothing happened. He laughed as She yelped in fear and stared at Him in disillusionment.

Even though He was aiming at the floor, a good distance

away from His young bride, She was terrified by the look of twisted pleasure in His eyes.

Pop!

Another false alarm. He began to tingle with excitement as She became more frightened. It was, in fact, Her fear that pushed Him to keep up the game. He had the power to keep Her hanging. Her only focus was on what He would do next, and this made Him blissfully happy. She saw Him wrap His finger around the trigger for another try, and She couldn't take it anymore. She had to get out of there.

She jumped up to get away; the sudden movement startled Him and broke His concentration.

Bang!

And a scream.

She felt the pain rip through Her legs and then She fell. When she regained Her composure, She looked down at Her foot. Composure was once again lost. Soap shrapnel covered the floor and mixed not-so-pleasantly with Her water that had just broken.

She didn't know what hurt worse: the swollen and throbbing toe, Her contracting uterus, or His maniacal laugh.

He helped Her up off the ground and lit a smoke.

"I guess we better get you to the hospital before that thing falls out on the floor."

Twelve hours later, that thing had a name—still no hope for a normal existence, but a name. I guess that's why I've always hated the name Kathleen. It was used all of my young life to address a situation, not a living person.

From the time of accidental conception, I was a situation. Those two young and rebellious misfits struggled to figure out how to deal with me, not care for me. Could They swaddle the infant and learn how to be alive in her presence? Or would she grow up just like Them—beaten, abused, and pawned?

Even though I have no memory of this event, I have a sense of place and time. People have identifying factors, events, lineages, and traces of past that tell the world who they are. This is who I am. It may not be outwardly apparent to those who casually know me, but some may notice the underlying frantic struggle to climb out from under the wreckage.

No Kathleen, There Isn't a Santa Claus

My heart was filled with Christmas hope. I knew that no matter how scary life could be, Santa could fix it. He would open that magic sack and out would explode the possibility of a better life—one without fear or pain. A life full of wonder, hope, and innocence was sure to arrive on this Christmas morning.

He must have felt the same way, because on that morning, He was in one of His good moods. It was the kind that let you know you had nothing to dread—at least for the time being.

I was on the floor, staring up into the brilliance of that moment. His hand was on Her shoulder, a grin on His face. He kissed Her as He rubbed Her, with all the assurance of a boy who had just found a dollar.

That was pretty much His outlook on life: *Wow! I found a buck! I'll spend it and feel great forever!* In truth, we all knew the meager value of a dollar and just held on to that moment as well as we could.

Money was tight. She sat on the worn sofa, heavy with yet another child, and hoped that He wouldn't take up bullet-making again anytime soon. The tree was tucked in the corner of the two-bedroom, basement apartment. The Christmas tree kind of resembled the weak Charlie Brown tree, but I knew this one wasn't going to turn into a glittering display anytime soon. I was hopeful but not operating under any illusion that this moment would last—not even at the tender age of four.

There were a few presents scattered under the tree. I suppose it was just enough to make the room a truly humble and realistic scene.

It is at this point that the details in my adult mind get sketchy. I must have opened my presents and marveled at the wonder and greatness of the man with the white beard. I do remember being warm and content in my pajamas, never wanting to leave the sanctity of that moment. She informed me, however, that it was time to get dressed to go to the Pleasant Place.

Why did I need to get dressed just to go upstairs? It didn't make any sense. But I knew not to argue.

She put my hair up in holiday fashion. Why did She do that? Every time we went somewhere, She would tease, rat, and mold my hair into a waspy beehive. I always looked like one of those overly made-up, beauty pageant kids.

When I was ready, looking creepy in a red velvet dress with a white collar, we headed upstairs. He had a glass in His hand that She suggested He leave at home.

"We're only going upstairs," He protested.

That stairway may as well have been a gateway into heaven, or at least into what most people's common perception of Christmas tranquility would be.

We were met with garland and gaiety, a mere glimpse of what was behind the door.

I always looked forward to going to the Pleasant Place. Even though it was just a flight of stairs away, the upstairs apartment had the air of a perfect life. Everything seemed in place. The mingled aroma of baked ham and Christmas cookies filled the rooms. There were presents everywhere. Twenty stockings hung at the chimney. Each had the name of the lucky recipient written in silver glitter. Everyone had one—grandmas, grandpas, aunts, uncles, cousins, in-laws, family pets, and extras, in case someone dropped by unexpectedly.

That was the beauty of the Pleasant Place: not one detail was left unattended to.

I came down from the initial surge of the magical experience when I noticed the presents. At first, they blended into the background of the Pleasant Place, and then the immensity of the stacks came to the forefront, lurching forward like a Christmas ghost.

My heart sank into the area of my stomach, where it was usually more at home. *Santa must have made a mistake. I've been so good*, I thought. Why did my bounty of Christmas cheer pale in comparison to the stacks in the Pleasant Place?

In fact, mine wasn't a bounty at all; mine was a buffer. It was only enough to field any questions. I guess They didn't want me to find out that my existence wouldn't be any more brilliant than the green ashtray that sat on the coffee table, filled to the brim with Kools and Salem's.

In the midst of my realistic decay, the Auspicious Adolescent approached. His look was oddly grim for one whose every whim was granted.

"What'd you get?" he asked.

I went to scratch my head and realized that my finger couldn't penetrate the molded nest on my head.

He noticed. "What happened to your hair?"

Well, I didn't know which question to answer first, so I responded with one of my own. "What did you get from Santa?" I asked.

"Hot Wheels Race Track, three different kinds of Lego sets, basketball and backboard, air hockey game, roller skates, 8-track player, ten new tapes, five new games, modeling clay, six shirts, three pairs of pajamas, a drum set, my own tool set, this cool pillow, GI Joe play set, four new GI Joe figures, six new action outfits, a stack of new Archie comics, and some other junk."

I just pointed—pointed toward the stacks of unopened treasures, wishing that by some fluke someone would reveal they were all for me. "If you already got all of those presents, who are these for?"

AA (Auspicious Adolescent) said, "That's the second opening. You know, for when the guests come. It's important that we have something to open."

The second opening proved joyous. I got a new Barbie. That was all I really cared about at the moment—that and the serene scene of a family coming together under the glistening foil tree.

The Pleasant Place mimicked a safe house. I could go there, bake cookies, get new toys, and be a floor away from the madness of my basement flat. This place, however, was a mirage. The Keeper was a prisoner left only to decorate as an attempt to escape her past and an uncertain future. The gifts were a way to spread happiness when there wasn't any to give. The whole place reeked of superficial responses to the sickness that overwhelmed the whole family.

As the color wheel turned, so did events. Alcohol seeped into the veins of the tranquility and thunder erupted. It seems He didn't like the way She seemed so happy in the arms of the relatives.

That night we learned exactly how frail our Christmas tree was. It couldn't withstand the force of Her being thrown into it. One of my new presents was broken, along with a few glasses, a lamp, Her flesh—in several different places—and my Christmas spirit.

Later that evening, after He had passed out, I asked Her why Santa brought so much more to the Pleasant Place. I don't know whether She was too broken to lie or if She thought the truth would set me free. Either way, it was on that Christmas night I learned there wasn't any Santa Claus.

As an adult, I have tried to reinvent my original hope in the happy elf, but the crashing of trees in my past keeps replaying. I put on a good show in order to not crush the spirits of my own children, but fear and disappointment still overwhelm the season.

In some sort of insane ritual, I guard the presents so that nothing tragic will happen to them or my children's Christmas hope. I move the wrapped treasures from the house to the garage, in case of fire, and then back into the house, in case of robbery. It is my feeble attempt to guard my home from the Christmas demons of my past. I suspect the Keeper of the Pleasant Place was trying to achieve the same goal. I'm just not sure if she fully understood the whole of her purpose.

The Basement

The basement is a scary place. The bottom level of this new home served as a replica of the darkest part of my soul. We moved two blocks away from the basement apartment and the Pleasant Place. Living above His parents somehow felt like an accomplishment and He bought fancy clothes to celebrate. He could take care of His aging parents and not pay rent. He indeed was moving up in the world.

I also achieved new status in the new home. At four and a half, I was a dutiful servant. Dragging the wash basket down the stairs, every thump brought me closer to that place I didn't want to go…especially by myself. The back stairs, in fact, were synonymous with a decent into doom.

The Elders worked during the day, and the lights were dim in the downstairs apartment. I somehow wished one of them would come out and accompany me down the stairs. However, their door, like an iron barricade, did not move, so I dragged the basket down to the patio.

How could such immense darkness prevail in the afternoon sun? The cement stairs lay ahead, mocking every movement forward I made. My heart pounded and my stomach ached with an unbound desire to get it over with.

I raced my fear into the basement. Hurriedly, I stuffed the clothes inside the washer, threw in some soap, pushed the buttons like I had been taught, and ran out with the basement demons at my feet. I reached the Elder's door and sat on the stairs to catch my breath. I had made it out but still wished that one of them would come out and share a reassuring hug.

It suddenly occurred to me that the trek up the stairs was equally as foreboding. I was too young to know why but could not escape the sense of dread.

There He was at the top of the stairs, smiling, and yet piercing me with His entombed rage.

"You dropped this," He said, reaching out to give me a black sock. "You'll have to go back down."

I knew better than to argue. After another foot race, I was back inside safely. But was I really safe?

The scene was far too similar to the week before when I was left outside during a tornado. Severe weather had prompted school officials to release us early in order to get us home before the storm set in.

My walker left me on the wrong side of the busy street as the sky turned green. She was just too scared to take me all the way to my door. Fear overwhelmed me as I tried to figure out how to get across the street. The forceful winds, however, encouraged me and I made it to my back door just as the tornado was overhead. I knocked, rang the bell, screamed, and pleaded, but no one answered. So there I stood, holding onto the door and hoping I wouldn't be swept away. The tornado was too loud and She and the inhabitants of the Pleasant Place couldn't hear me from their safe haven in the basement.

It seems funny that the place I was so afraid of would also be the place I wished I could be at that moment. Maybe the basement itself, with all of the cracked walls and cobwebs, wasn't the origin of my fear—like now, when the thought of the swirling, summoning winds of a tornado are not what send me into panic whenever the sky turns green.

When kids are scared, they yearn for their moms and dads to sweep them up into safety. I didn't feel safe anywhere, and now the Pleasant Place was too far away to run to on my own. At least the basement there was closer to heaven. At least a common idea of heaven: as a place that is beautiful and untouched by ugliness. I didn't know what I did to be sent to Hell, but I felt guilty. And thus the basement symbolized both my yearning for escape and my solitude in this life.

No Daddy, Don't Go

My room was at the top level of the house and what would seem like miles away from the basement. The ascent was similar to a climb up the stairwell of an office building. Each floor had a purpose. The basement was where the demons resided. The Elders lived on the first floor and held the deed to the house and the keys to keep His behavior somewhat in check. Her beauty parlor was housed on the main floor, and the top level was where we slept off the perils of the day.

There had always been a beauty parlor in our house. Unlike the wet bars that had always shared our living space, the shampoo sink and the hair dryers represented a link to the American dream. Ladies of all shapes and sizes would stop in each week to be coiffed and curled. In return, I received a glimpse of the real world and acquired a bunch of pseudo-grandmas.

That was Her contribution to the household economy, as well as the beautification of the northwest side of Chicago. I loved to watch Her in that place. Cutting hair, it seemed, was Her purpose. Even now, years later, people still come from miles around to participate in Her mastery of the art.

I loved the beauty shop. It was the safest place in our house. As long as the clientele was about, He had to be on His best behavior. The women, strangely enough, loved Him. There was this charm and quit wit He had that seemed to entrance people. I liked it, too. I secretly wished that the beauty shop were always open.

One day, upon returning from the Pleasant Place, I found the beauty parlor closed, the dryers quiet, and my safety net severed. She sat in the dark cutting her hair. Because I had seen Her do this most of my young life, it came as no surprise to see the mirrors strategically placed so that She could see the back.

"Why don't you have someone do that for you?" I asked.

"No one can do it the way I like it," She replied.

As I watched, there seemed to be a sense of urgency to the way She slid the scissors along Her bangs. She must have seen the inquiry on my face and realized She was in full view among the surrounding mirrors.

"Go clean your room," She blurted in such a way that I knew She didn't want me around anymore.

Something took over my senses, and I felt the word spill out like the cup of milk I'd knocked over a week before. I remembered the milk because He had swept all of the dishes, food, and everything else from the table onto the floor in an insane rage. The milk hadn't even touched His food, but I guess it must have interrupted the sanctity of His dinnertime ritual, which consisted of manhattans and meat. I'm convinced this is why I'm now a vegetarian.

The word was "*No!*"

I don't know why I said it, but the damage had been done. She got up from the chair, and with fire in Her eyes She screamed, "What did you say to me? *Don't ever let me hear that word come out of your mouth again!*"

And then She proceeded to chase me all over the beauty shop until I finally hid behind one of the dryers. She reached down and pulled me out by my hair. Then I was marched to the bathroom to have my mouth washed out with soap—it was the seventies, people really did that kind of thing back then.

We later had a conversation about how the AA had influenced my bad decision, and that spending too much time in the Pleasant Place was clouding the reality of my gritty existence.

I fell asleep that night with the taste of Dove lingering in my mouth and I remember being woken abruptly by the sound of Her pleading. Sneaking down to the front hall with the phone in my hand, I went to see if the Chicago police were due for a visit.

He was trying to leave, and oddly enough, She was trying to stop Him. I heard something about Him wanting to get out and the woman who was going to bring Him peace. She was pulling Him by the arm and pleading. My dilemma protruded from the scene like a mountain in the distance. We would all be better off without Him—no more fear, no more fighting, no more...

Instead of waving goodbye, my hand clung to Hers and we pulled. She screamed, "*No!*"

My mouth opened, but the coating of Dove soap caught the word I was no longer allowed to murmur, ever.

This word still chokes me. It's not the taste of the Dove that stops the protest, it's more the fear of what will happen by saying no—by telling Him to stop, by screaming in agony for the pain to go away. None of this was allowed. It was like He was the only one allowed to be in pain. Everyone should notice His pain, His grief, and His helplessness. We were all supposed to forgive Him because He couldn't forgive Himself. I'd almost feel sorry for Him except that He tortured us.

He was torturing Her now. He probably didn't intend to leave for good. Watching us beg and plead made Him feel powerful.

&)(&

He came back the next day, and restored the instability that wheezed life into our family.

She Looks Funny, Let's Throw Glass at Her

My academic career began in a half-day kindergarten at the local public school. She didn't drive, so my adventure began on a blue, lady's bike with baskets on the back. I would sit on the back of the bike and put my feet in the baskets.

My only enrichment thus far had been from the beauty shop ladies and a book that my godfather had bought for my birthday. I could read that book verbatim. Some insisted that it was because I had memorized the words.

It was true. Robert McCloskey's words were etched in my brain like the recipe for manhattans. I understood them and could recognize other words, as well. The story was completely unreal to me yet utterly compelling. In *Blueberries for Sal*, she and her mom went berry picking and then canned jam for the long winter. I loved the way that Little Sal and her mom carried on this tradition. Even when Little Sal encountered a bear on the berry picking trip, she wasn't afraid. I suppose this is because she didn't live with a grizzly bear and knew that her mom would never let anything bad happen to her.

Storytelling was fascinating to me, and I yearned to capture every moment. I would dream about making jam while stirring the vermouth and listening to the ice cubes clink in the glass. I also wondered if Little Sal was a boy or a girl. These thoughts, however, ended up locked in the Black Room with my spirit.

I must have been scared to be in that place, with children who were alive with hope. They knew instantly that I was different and avoided me like a school salami sandwich. Two children in particular caught my attention. These two were beauties. Blonde hair, blue eyes, and clothes right out of the Sears Wish Book. To me, children like this only existed in the movies. I named them, affectionately, the Chitty Chitty Bang Bang Girl and the Chitty Chitty Bang Bang Boy. I couldn't believe that I was sitting next to them in the circle. Each child shared relevant facts about themselves. The movie stars were twins and had a nanny and a housekeeper. They also spent their summer vacations at Disney Land and the beach.

It was my turn to share some facts about myself.

Should I share the recipe for manhattans? Would they like to know that Santa was made up? Perhaps the story of my birth?

The teacher beckoned. "Kathleen, Kathleen, it your turn."

I opened my mouth and threw up.

The janitor came with the orange-smelling sawdust and She was called. As I rode home in the baskets, I could still hear their voices yelling "yuck" and I could still feel the

Chitty Chitty Bang Bang Boy and Girl getting up to run away from me. I somehow knew that school would be much like home.

The next day I awoke with a stomachache but was forced to go to school anyway. When I sat in the circle, I could still smell the orange-smelling sawdust. In fact, I can still smell it today. No one would sit by me. There it began: my entry into social isolation, my introduction to schoolyard harassment.

That day on the playground, the kids stayed away from me. There was no mention of the incident, but the Chitty Chitty Bang Bang Girl and the Chitty Chitty Bang Bang Boy asked me if I was sick. My reply was a mumbled "yesterday."

"No! We mean those circles under your eyes. What's wrong with you, anyway?"

I started to tell them that He had shot Her with a soap bullet, and that I'd been born prematurely, but such things didn't happen in the world of Chitty Chitty Bang Bang.

The next day, I was dubbed Circle Girl.

This is my fondest memory of kindergarten. Nothing to etch into a memory book, but one takes what one gets and runs with it.

And run I did—through the tattered playground of my existence. No one played with me. Who could blame them? I was different. It's funny how children can see what adults either don't or choose to walk away from.

My academic experiences sprouted from the seed of my first day of school, much like my life experiences were spawned from the horror of my birth. The next big event took place in second grade.

There I was, standing alone on the playground with my nose pressed against the window, waiting to come in, when I felt something hit my hand. I looked down, expecting to brush off whatever it was. What happened next was like a scene out of *Carrie*, and that movie hadn't even been filmed yet.

It's funny how much I loved that movie. I would marvel at the way Carrie's mom would lock her in the crawl space. In a sense, Carrie was my hero. Isolated, broken, but ready to wreak havoc on the society that had done her wrong.

So, I raised my bloody hand, and to my surprise, my middle knuckle was as exposed as the blood vessels beneath my eyes. Someone had thrown glass at me. Now that I think about it, this is why I was so scared at the end of *Carrie* when the bloody hand came out of the ground. It brought back the bloody recollections of my playground days.

I rushed to the playground teacher, Mrs. Gerkowitcz. Yep, that was her name. I'm not sure why I remember it, but I guess you don't forget a name like that. I hope that she and Carrie don't ask for royalties, because they will remain the only two players in this drama to be called by their real names.

Mrs. Gerkowitcz freaked out and pulled me quickly into the office. She acted quickly, just like Miss Collins in *Carrie*, who stopped all of the girls from throwing tampons at Carrie in the locker room. If only my adversaries had thrown tampons instead of glass, I wouldn't have needed stitches. I can still remember the doctor telling me that the stitches would dissolve like they were never even there.

My right hand, however, still bears the scar that reaches across my knuckles. It comes in handy for telling my right hand from my left. I could have used that scar during my kindergarten graduation.

I'd held my right fist closed tight so I would remember to accept my diploma with the correct hand. How proud I'd been, thinking no one would be able to make fun of me, and I could make fun of them if they used the wrong hand. With more cockiness than I'd ever displayed before, I'd reached out to get my diploma. The principal had bent down—to congratulate me, I thought—and gently tapped my other hand. I still can't figure out how I'd gotten the two mixed up. The Chitty Chitty Bang Bang Boy and Girl had just laughed.

As I got older, people stopped asking how I got that scar. It must have been because there were bigger wounds to investigate.

Why Do You Have Grass in Your Living Room

There was a boy in the fourth grade. I call him Artist Boy. Every time we were to draw or create, Artist Boy would scribble out something that became the envy of us all. The Head Mistress would coo and praise his every effort. I hated him for it. Any of my own self-expressions came out muddled and stark. At the time, I wasn't aware of the saying "art imitates life." However, I did know that in my house, we weren't supposed to take pride in anything.

Whenever the Younger Set or I tried to show off a piece of work to Him, the comment was always the same. "That's creative, all right. Just like tits on a bull." That saying became etched in my brain. I never really understood what it meant, but the implication was clear. I would sometimes try to picture what the bull would look like with a set of tits. That only confused me further.

Anyway, She always did my art homework for me. She could draw, paint, and create better than even Artist Boy. Because She had never received Her own praise, She would revel in our amazement of Her creations.

This day in class, however, I did not have the option of having someone do it for me. The assignment was to draw a picture of a room in our house. I drew, erased, started over, and started over again. I looked over at Artist Boy and saw the beginnings of an interior masterpiece. Just for once, I thought, I have to beat him. Why should he always get all of the attention?

So, with all of the creative energy that I could find, I drew what I thought was the most beautiful picture of our living room. Every detail was laid down onto that piece of construction paper. At one point the Head Mistress came by and said, "Kathleen, I like the way that you are working." I felt it! Pride! It was wonderful and gave me the spark to finish my creation. I looked back at Artist Boy, and he was finished. A crowd of fourth graders surrounded him, marveling at the genius of the bookcases in his picture. I didn't care, although I secretly imagined them coming to me and oohing and ahhing over my carpet.

Yes! The carpet, to me, was the best part of the living room. This wasn't the carpet from my own living room. In my picture, I drew the plush, green shag that adorned the parlor of the Pleasant Place. She wouldn't let me call the room "the parlor," however, because She said it sounded like a funeral. So, in my house we called it the front room. Well, the carpet in the front room was beaten and full of cigarette burns. I couldn't turn in that picture. Besides, how could the Head Mistress deny a beautiful drawing of the Pleasant Place? I knew that she and the class would love it.

In the picture, I was there playing with my Barbies with a ray of light coming through the thick, paisley curtains. I was smiling. I was the only one in the room and the solitude was peaceful. For once, I was not scared. He could not come into this world I had created. Not Him or a bull with tits.

I pranced to the front of the room with picture in hand and waited my turn. Each child before me showed the Head Mistress their picture and beamed from the rave reviews. My anticipation was growing as I came to the second place in line.

Finally, it was my turn. I handed my picture to the Head Mistress, and there was silence. I thought that it must have been so good she was rendered speechless.

She spoke one word, "Grass?" and then there was more. "Why do you have grass in your living room?"

I spoke quietly. "It's not grass; it's shag carpeting."

"Well it looks like grass. Go fix it!" She tossed the picture at me and sent me back to my desk with my classmates all mocking my efforts.

"We should have known that she would have grass in her living room."

Artist Boy looked smug but also a little sad for me.

I took a black crayon and scribbled out the shag. I should have known that one cannot replace their own reality with the luxuries of others'.

Bullets

My homework one evening was to write sentences for English class. This was a task I took great pleasure in. I loved the way words came together to form a collective statement of creativity. As I reached the end of my assigned list of words, there was a word that escaped my understanding. I asked Her if She knew what "serenity" meant. She stated that She had never heard the word before and couldn't even begin to tell me what it meant. She suggested I look it up in the dictionary.

I loved that dictionary! It must have weighed ten pounds, was unabridged, and seemed to hold all of the mysteries of the universe in it. Equally entrancing to my curious, pre-adolescent soul was the frankness of the profane language terms. Sometimes I would take it off of the shelf to wonder at the audacity of the publisher who dared to define the native language of my parents and extended family. All of the words in there gave generic descriptions of our immoral existence, and this somehow made me feel normal.

As I cruised into the living room to grab the book off of the shelf, I tiptoed past the sleeping monster. He had been in an explosive mood this day and I was grateful that His self-medication had, at least temporarily, tamed the beast. With the magic book in hand, I headed back to my assignment. Eagerly, I flipped through the pages until I reached the *s*'s. Then, my excitement turned to disappointment. Right where serenity should be, there was a large bullet hole.

Now, I was completely aware that the hole existed. It had been there for years, fracturing all of the words in its path. This evening, however, I suddenly grew angry at the realization that my beloved dictionary was also the helpless victim of His unsightly rage.

This was only one of many bullet holes in our home, and I guess I should have been thankful that they were only super-ficial wounds in the furnishings. I found the damage almost laughable, and would invite people over to see the hole in the floor that oozed light from the basement. There were three other books that had taken the force of His pistol. However, they were more forgettable, due to our lack of interest in the *Time Life* cooking series and the *Encyclopaedia Britannica*.

Running my fingers over the pierced pages, I tried to re-member the night of the fatal incident. We knew that His five gun collection could claim a victim at any time. I guess, like all of the other atrocities, we just tried to ignore the inevitable. As I made up a sentence for serenity (*I went to the neighbor's house to borrow a cup of serenity*), the scene began to replay in my mind.

It was a Saturday night, and They were playing cards, laughing out loud, watching *M*A*S*H*, and drinking heavily. The room was filled with the scents of perfume, cigarette smoke, Canadian Club, combined with the lingering aroma of the smoked butt that we had had for dinner. This was the norm for our quality, family time. I had loved to watch Her laugh at the show and fawn over Alan Alda. I would enjoy the moment as if it were the last to come for awhile. The Younger Set had already been sent off to bed, leaving me to keep watch over the lovebirds.

It was at that point that She made a horrible mistake.

She won the card game.

"You cheated!" He yelled. That yell, which sounded like the gurgling, last gulp of air that one would emit when drowning, sent me crawling toward my room. The last thing I saw before I escaped was the look in His eyes. In comparison, that stare resembled the look of someone who is also about to take their last living breath—urgent, painful, and one moment closer to death. He must have been painfully aware that every breath he took could be his last. When someone is not meant to inhabit the earth, this may be the only particle of self-realization they even subconsciously possess. Then, to Him human life was nothing more than an alcoholic binge. I heard the card table being turned over and Her pathetic attempt to escape the scene. The bathroom door locked and I let my breath go, feeling that She would be safe, at least for the moment. I held the phone in my hand and grappled with the decision to call the police. That was never easy for me. If I didn't call, She could die at His hand, and if I did call, I could be the next victim. I heard small sobs coming from the Younger Set and peeked in to see if I could help. They were huddled together in the bottom bunk, holding each other as if the embrace could shield them from His wrath.

Silence.

The lack of sound was paralyzing. All we could do was sit there and wait. Again we were helpless as we listened to the footsteps coming down the hall with the fierceness of a staggering bull. He called to Her in a singsong voice, almost pleading for Her to come out. She refused, and then the sound of the gun sent me plunging into the bottom bunk.

The police decision had been made.

I whispered into the phone, "I think He shot my mom."

The Younger Set sobbed and He garbled, "Shut up and go to sleep."

The police had left with one of His guns after Her refusal to press charges. He then retreated to rest His weary trigger finger. She fell asleep in the middle of the floor as if the life had been sucked from Her, and the Younger Set finally went back to sleep. And there I'd been, awake and in charge of the aftermath.

During my sweep of the room to make sure all of the cigarettes were out and the doors were locked, I'd spied the fallen dictionary on the shelf. It had been on its side with particles of the English language surrounding it. In essence, its guts had been blown out. I'd swept the remains into my trembling hand, kissed Her bruised cheek, and closed my bedroom door and disappeared into the Black Room.

The Black Room served as a vault for every horrific experience that fell upon me. It was not until twenty years later, during intense therapy, that I would have to revisit this place. I remember the fear upon reentrance and the pain associated with clearing away the debris. The excavation, however, was necessary in order to create my own definition for serenity.

You Look Like You Need a Friend

I magine having a whole collection of deep, dark secrets and no one to share them with. Kids avoided me like the plague; and why not? I looked sick, I felt sick most of the time, and my social skills were ill at best. Sure, there were one or two girls who felt sorry for me and would hang around with me once in a while, but no one ever wanted to come to my house. It was like they knew about the evil that lurked there. A family down the street—the Missing-and-Crooked-Teeth Family—would come around, but I think that they had been humbled to a new sort of oblivion. They would come to call. Yes, just like Mayberry. One would stand outside your house and yell "Yo" and your name. If you were free, you would come out. Sometimes, He would answer the call, and they would run back down the street to the safety of their own misery. It's funny what the human mind retains, or what becomes relevant in the aftermath.

The only memories of the social life that I had have been recorded in this publication. I don't remember anything about sixth grade—nothing! No names, no faces. I do, however, have some pretty clear memories about seventh grade and some folks I met along the way. This group (along with the AA) saw to it that I received the kind of attention that I had come to think I deserved.

I'm not sure how it started. I seem to remember a note written to Johnny Sweetface saying I liked him and asking if he would go out with me. Well, of course he knew what a preposterous request this was. I, in my naïvety, thought he was a good choice.

Not only was I a social outcast, but I had bad fashion sense—which She both inspired and sewed for me—and I had also gained some pubescent weight. I was ugly. No, this wasn't a perception of myself, it was a fact. Girls that age tend to be awkward, but I was wayward. I'm sure She thought She was doing enough to help me along, but She had no clue. I was fat, clumsy, had no fashion sense, and had bad hair thanks to what a woman who was stuck in her own youth thought was appropriate for a seventh grade girl in the seventies.

What I wanted more than anything was to fit in. Not a surprise for most girls my age, but for me it was an attempt to make my horrible existence worth living. I would do anything for acceptance, and I did.

The first initiation into my new social circle came in the way of a drug deal, of sorts. Johnny Sweetface asked if I wanted to buy some joints. I didn't really know what this involved, but these joints would be my ticket into the good life. I asked, "how much?"

Two dollars apiece was the set price. I went home that night and emptied my bank. The next day I traveled to school with a new set of platform shoes and the cash that would buy my way into their hearts. I clutched the money much like I had clutched the kindergarten diploma in my left hand.

My head was held high; this was my day. I felt fashionable and flamboyant because of the impending deal. Then, while crossing the street into the playground, I tripped. My ankle gave out and I ended up sprawled in the middle of the street with my cash scattered around me. The crossing guard yelled at me to get up, and in my haste and embarrassment, I lost one of my dollars.

Kids on the corner yelled, "Why don't you learn to walk in those shoes?" I suddenly hated those shoes and vowed never to wear them again. I plodded on, however, just like I was programmed to do.

As soon as I got into the room, I told Johnny Sweetface I had the money. "Not now!" he snapped.

After lunch he told me to meet him in the playground after school.

There we were, all alone. This was the defining moment of seventh grade. I had hoped someone would see me with him so I could be the talk of the school on Monday. He gave me the joints and I gave him the money. I asked him if I could kiss him. He said maybe another time, and told me that we could arrange it after I tried the joints.

They were wrapped in strawberry paper and smelled delicious. I had already been smoking cigarettes, so I thought this would be just like that.

That night, we visited Her mother and father's house. I chose the basement bathroom for my smoking room. I kept trying to light the joints, but every time I took a long drag, it would go out. The aroma was something like burning leaves. Since I hadn't had any experience with this before, I assumed this was normal. At one point, I unwrapped one of the joints to inspect its contents. It looked like leaves. Not typical cannabis leaves, but more like ones you would find on your backyard oak tree. Could my Johnny Sweetface have deceived me? I would have to wait until Monday. I tried to act high, but to no avail; I was still just me and there was no escaping it.

I spent the rest of the evening trying to explain what I was doing in the bathroom and where the smell of burning leaves was coming from.

Falling asleep that night, I dreamt of Johnny's Sweetface and how it would feel against mine.

In a pair of flat shoes, I met Johnny Sweetface on the playground Monday morning. He asked me if I felt like an Indian. Not understanding his implication, I simply stated that I hadn't caught a buzz. "Most people can't get high off of tree leaves," he chuckled.

Later in class, he asked me to unbutton my blouse one button. I did it. I felt sexy, and I forgot about the fact that he had ripped me off and ridiculed me. He asked for another button. I was on fire; I did it. He said he would consider going out with me, but we could talk about it later at my house.

On Second Thought

The beauty parlor was closed. Hair dryers, shampoo bowls, and caddies of rollers, however, still remained. She had decided getting out of the house would be an advantageous move. I think it was because of His decision about another advantageous move.

After His father had died, all agreed that we should buy a house with His mother. We were told we would have to take care of her now. This meant he would be keeping the free rent agreement and obtaining a part of His dad's estate while His mom was still alive. Now there were funds for barhopping, Dunhill lighters, and leather sports coats. She still had to work, however, and we still ate SPAM and wore homemade clothes. The Younger Set and I were second-class citizens, and we were reminded of this constantly.

I somehow didn't mind doing all of the yard work and carrying His Mother's groceries up to the second floor. This house had a much nicer bar, and I was now acquainted with Johnny Sweetface, the one who would make my adolescent dreams come true. Anyway, He was always happier with money clenched in His fist; and with His mommy dearest around, He wasn't quite so volatile.

The problem was that His mom constantly berated Her. No matter how hard She worked, it was never good enough. She would always be the one who had taken the son away from the mother.

So, in Her first move toward independence, She took a job in someone else's beauty shop. I liked it when She went to work. It meant more work for me, but I was free from Their intolerance of each other. And I now had the beauty shop to myself. I would go downstairs and sit in the dark and watch my silhouette in the large mirror. I looked good in silhouette. You couldn't tell I had a stupid haircut and dark circles under my eyes. I didn't even look as fat in the dark. I would sometimes take off some of my clothes and marvel at how good I looked in the dark. I betted that if Johnny Sweetface could see me in the dark, he would think I was girlfriend material.

The next day at school, he told me I might be worthy of his attention. My heart jumped. He then informed me that if his friend liked me, I could go out with the guy. If that worked out okay, then good ol' Johnny Sweetface would consider being my beau. The plan was that Johnny Sweetface and his friend, Smooth Leo, would come to my house after school, and I would ask Smooth Leo out.

I was apprehensive, but what did I have to lose? The dating game took place in the beauty shop. Johnny Sweetface served as the advisor. He told me that when I had unbuttoned my shirt in class, he'd thought I was beautiful, and this should be the first step in attracting Smooth Leo. I turned off the lights in the beauty shop and unbuttoned my blouse until it gaped open. I was careful not to open it too much, so my chubby belly didn't show. Then, I unhooked my bra. This was a move that always drove AA crazy. Anytime he requested it, I complied, and he became my servant. AA would always ask for more and would promise anything in return.

I loved that power. And realizing I had the power, I knew doing this would bring me closer to Johnny Sweetface.

So, there I was in the shampoo chair with my breasts out in the open. I put one hand on my left breast, and at the same time, Johnny Sweetface walked in to check my pose. He was surprised at my audacity, but said it was perfect. Smooth Leo walked in and said he liked what he saw. He asked me if I would move my pants down past my knees. This scared me, but AA usually liked it. So I thought, "why not?"

Smooth Leo dropped his pants. His dick was rock-hard and much bigger than AA's. He told me to take off my pants and come over and kiss him. I did it, but as I came close and parted my lips to meet his, he pointed to his hard-on. I began to protest, but then I saw Johnny Sweetface standing at the door. He told me to remember what the payoff would be. I so wanted to be with him, so I got down on my knees and proceeded to kiss Smooth Leo's dick. He said I should suck on it like a lollipop. I tried but gagged several times. At that moment we heard footsteps upstairs and had to close the party.

The Long and Winding Road

Grandma was dead. I seem to recall a funeral and much sadness coming from the Keeper of the Pleasant Place. He, however, drank His way through the mourning period. And then there was the inheritance.

When He had money, He was on top of the world. Top-shelf whiskey replaced the cheap stuff, we moved out of her house, and for the first time in Their lives, They owned something. The new house needed lots of work, and there was the matter of installing the wet bar. Soon enough, our new home was available for living, or the beginning of a new chapter.

Now, in eighth-grade, I had to switch schools. No more after-school fellatio festivals. I tried to say goodbye to Johnny Sweetface, but he was grieving over the death of his new girlfriend, who had been abducted, raped, and murdered. I sucked his dick once more, for old times' sake, and began to fret over a whole new social emergency.

It was two months before graduation, and my new class-mates had no interest in befriending an overweight misfit. I just tried to blend in as best as I could. There wasn't even any-one interested in a blowjob. I didn't advertise, but I looked for prospects. During the second day of my initiation, I saw a familiar face. I looked her way and she looked mine. We both knew that, somehow, we had met before, but were not sure how. Being blonde, beautiful, self-assured, and curious, she ap-proached me. "Don't I know you?" she asked.

"I don't know," I replied. "Have you always gone to school here?"

She said she had been there since second grade. I asked her where she went to school when she was little. I was shocked to find out she had gone to the same school I had for Kindergar-ten through fifth grade.

Oh my God! There she was in living color—The Chitty Chitty Bang Bang Girl. This was too surreal. The weirdest part was that she was talking to me like we had been friends for all of this time. I was elated. This was the birth of my first friendship. She was excited to have a friend from her past and began to tell everyone we had been best friends since kindergarten. I knew it wasn't true, but who was I to refuse companionship?

No one in the new school liked me except the Chitty Chitty Bang Bang Girl. I don't think even she really liked me. She was just attracted to the nostalgia of our relationship. Whatever the reason, I didn't complain and enjoyed our interactions. I told her about Johnny Sweetface, Smooth Leo, and AA. She told me she had only French-kissed a boy and would like to learn from me. Imagine me teaching the Chitty Chitty Bang Bang Girl how to suck cock. Before that event could occur, she asked me if I wanted to go to church with her.

Church sounded like an alien place to me. I only remembered going with the Keeper of the Pleasant Place occasionally. People knelt a lot in Catholic churches. Before you could enter a pew, you had to bless yourself and then kneel. Only then could you be accepted into God's world. I did it but felt strange, like I was sinning because the blessing was backward. I also felt like God didn't like me much anyway, and that I must have pissed him off in some way in order to have my kind of life.

The Chitty Chitty Bang Bang Girl told me she went to church at night, and it wasn't like the Catholic Church at all. Her club was called CHUMS. I think it was an acronym for something, but I can't recall what. Anyway, I loved it! Everyone welcomed me, and not one person asked me to take my clothes off or told me that I was special like tits on a bull. This place was all right. We did crafts, read bible quotes, sang songs, and learned how to earn the big CHUMS reward. I guess I am sketchy on some of the details, but what I do remember very clearly is that I was loved in this place. I felt safe, special, and like I had been personally introduced to God. And guess what? This God did like me and did not think I was evil because I threw away a funfair bible or ate an extra communion wafer.

I walked home on the very cloud given to me by the CHUMS God. I floated, felt, and forgot about the horror that awaited me at home. I was free from all of the evil that had condemned me from the moment of my inception. I was even excited to go home and tell Them about my experience. I wanted Them to know that I felt good—really good—and that I hadn't felt this good ever.

Then, all at once, I was startled from my spiritual sanctity. I looked down the block and saw Him in the middle of the sidewalk, standing there like a madman. What was He doing? *Oh my CHUMS God*, could He be waiting for me? I knew I hadn't done anything wrong. But, maybe I had.

As I got closer, He started yelling. *"Where the hell have you been?* Don't you know that it is 7:30 on a school night, and you are out running the streets? What have you been doing? Screwing some guys? You whore! Get in the fucking house!"

And He kicked me. He kicked me so hard I fell on the cement stairs and cut open my knee. At that point, She had heard the commotion and my screaming and ran out to see what was going on.

"She was at church!" She yelled. I had never seen Her talk to Him like that before. That was the first time I had ever seen Her stick up for one of us. She told me to go inside. I just ran to my room and sobbed. I was mourning the loss of my CHUMS God. I had only known him for a short time but knew that if we had had some time together, we would have become life-long friends.

He, of course, never said He was sorry, but also didn't continue the beating. Strangely enough, I only recall one other time that He ever hit me. Through all of His psychotic behavior, He only hit Her. This night, however, it was me. It was like He knew He was going to lose his hold on me and was somehow jealous of the CHUMS God, even though He didn't know about him yet. It was like He knew I was coming home with *good news*, and this headline would have been too much for His feeble mind to bear.

ഓര

Well, the day had finally arrived: Graduation. Yes, I would finally be free from social persecution and the horrors of my elementary education. But first, I had to find a dress.

This was not going to be easy. I had gained more weight and had lost the hope of ever being beautiful. She had cut my hair in a Dorothy Hamil type of style. That was the last thing I needed—a haircut that made my face look paler and my nose bigger. This look would certainly add to my already non-flattering physique. To top it off, I needed a gown. She took me shopping, and after trying to squeeze into at least forty dresses, I actually found one I liked. It was light and flowing with long sleeves that draped over my hands. I kind of looked like Stevie Nicks, although I didn't know who she was at the time. We capped off the outfit with a pair of cork platforms (even though I had sworn I would never wear them again) and a pearl necklace. I actually looked pretty good, and She even offered to help me put on some makeup for the event.

When I arrived at the auditorium, I saw the Chitty Chitty Bang Bang Girl and went up to hug her. She looked more beautiful than I had ever seen. Her dress was white and lacy and her hair was pulled back with a ribbon. She looked a virgin about to be offered for sacrifice.

She looked at me and began to give the obligatory "you look nice" when she noticed my dress. She had a look of horror in her eyes. Did I really look that bad?

"I'm your friend, right?" she said. I just looked at her perplexed. "Anyway, you're going to find out eventually." She pointed across the room to one of our classmates—who was wearing my dress. I shrank. Why was it that whenever I felt good, something happened to screw it up?

This girl, whom I will call Copy Cat, came up to me and said, "Nice going. Leave it to you to copy my dress. You've ruined my day!" And she stomped off. Of course I felt bad, like it was my fault. Just another day.

It was time to get on stage and sing our song. Someone had chosen "The Long and Winding Road." I had never heard the song before we began practicing it, but I didn't mind it so much and it was kind of catchy. So we began to sing, and the Chitty Chitty Bang Bang Girl grabbed my hand and we cried while singing:

Has left a pool of tears crying for the day.

Why leave me standing here, let me know the way.

I don't know why I was crying; it's just that I heard people do this during graduation, so I thought I better fit in. I kept forcing tears until they came. At that moment there was only me and the Chitty Chitty Bang Bang Girl, and we were moving on up in the world.

After the ceremony, there was a party. We went to dinner at an Italian restaurant, which pissed Him off because He didn't really like Italian food—and why would He want to sit around with a bunch of Wops, anyway? Because He was already not happy, He drank heavily. This is all I remember about the party besides the money I received. I was told it was all mine and that I only had to save some of it.

He got so loaded and belligerent that She left to take Her parents home. I can't believe She left the Younger Set and me alone with Him. I guess She thought the Keeper of The Pleasant Place would look after us. But she had a stomachache and left, too.

Well, He decided it was time to go. He looked at me and said, "I can't drive, so you're going to get us home. After all you're a grown up now that you've graduated."

I pleaded with Him, but He insisted I get in the car and drive home. The Younger Set began to cry, but I told them it would be okay and not to worry. I got behind the wheel and froze. How was I going to get this car and my family home safely? I think I must have asked the CHUMS God for help. Then, I began to navigate the car down the long and winding road.

Follow in the Footsteps

In the matter of academics, I have always had some luck. Assignments and homework were effortless and easy for me. I was an honor roll student who wasn't sure how she got there. Because of this and my Iowa test scores, I was placed in one of the top high schools in the Chicago area. Of course, I had no clue how this school was going to affect me. I had not yet experienced the sensation of being on top.

I got on the bus that first morning sick and afraid. In a way, I was happy all of the atrocities of elementary school were behind me, but I feared a whole new set of ill interactions awaited. I knew it was going to be a long ride into the heart of the city. Never had I been so far from home on my own before. Thinking back, I did not understand why I had to do it alone. Who would send their daughter out alone into the world without even a sack lunch?

They would, and did.

As I got off the bus and looked at my new school, I was overwhelmed by the institutional labyrinth that stood before me. I somehow knew I would never make it there, so I entered as a temporary tenant of higher education. The first place I had to go was to my homeroom classroom. I found it easily, and for a moment I felt comfortable in this place. That is, until I saw her—Mrs. Tub-O-Lard. She was old, dark, and mean. Every word that squirmed from her eating orifice was contradictory, condescending, and cold. Honestly, Mrs.Tub-O-Lard was almost as scary as Him. At least I only had to spend ten minutes a day with her.

After surviving homeroom, I got lost on my way to algebra. I ended up being ten minutes late and was pegged a troublemaker. This was too bad, because I had so wanted to go there and be an ideal, a cheerleader, a homecoming queen. What I would end up as, however, was a product of my parents. I was too fat to be a cheerleader, anyway. And I think that you had to be pretty and popular to be a homecoming queen, so that was out as well. Maybe I would find a group that would consider me an ideal. That thought is what carried me through the rest of the day.

At lunch, in the cafeteria, I had hoped to find my clique. This may sound too much like an episode of *Square Pegs*, but I admit to getting lost in that show's reality. It is true that misfits find each other and make other misfits, but the misfit gene pool is weak, and they never triumph and take over the world. As I remember, that series ended with the square pegs still outward and outcast.

I tried to look like I knew what I was doing, but I dropped my cheeseburger and was left lunch-less. Someone commented that I didn't need the food anyway.

I knew I would never make it in the cafeteria, so after a few days of investigating, I found out that students could leave campus for lunch. The only problem was, freshman weren't allowed to participate.

On the last day of my first week of high school, I snuck out and ate at Mc Donald's with the upperclassmen and rule-breakers. Here, I would find my clique.

These kids were goal-orientated; just what I needed. How long could I emulate my parental role models and still make it in the normal world? The creed of the group was not to be *academically* superior, but to beat the system.

Well, it's not always wise to stray from the home front, anyway.

I was quickly introduced to our first goal: to stay in Mc-Donald's as long as you could without buying more than a diet soda and without getting kicked out for loitering.

We could usually make it until 10:30, or so, but then were put out to attend classes. This was far from the plan, so we had to find somewhere else to go. The team leader had found the best secret hiding place. This was a path under the bridge and along the banks of the river. We could stay there dodging river rats until the first lunch period began at 11:10. Forty minutes of adventure seemed to outweigh forty minutes of algebra, so this became the daily plan. Once students filed into the restaurant for lunch, we could stay until the end of the day. All lunch periods were finished by 1:15, and then some upper classmen were out of school for the day, so the managers would let us stay. The managers knew we were cutting class but obviously had no problem with our loitering. We could basically spend all day at McDonald's except for one hour in the morning. I don't understand how the restaurant would be liable for kids skipping school, but we didn't question it and just stuck to the schedule. Of course, you would have to show up to classes once in awhile so no one would call your house to see where you were.

This would be the group's first matter of discussion upon meeting in the morning at McDonald's. We would all be wondering if anyone got busted for cutting. This was a big fear that was instilled by the school. During our freshman orientation and everyday from then, students were reminded about the strict attendance code the school followed. We were told parents would be called the first day of student absence and that they would have to sign a reinstatement after three days. We got around some of this by sneaking back into the school for a meeting with our advisory period, or division, as it was called. As long as you could make division, parents would not usually be called.

On any given day, I could find one or two people to skip school with. There were about ten of us and each person would skip one or two days each week. I, however, got addicted to skipping school. That's just what I needed—another bad habit. I was so happy to not have to go. School had always been a nightmare, and now I was making the choice not to be involved. I had never had a choice in whether or not to be exposed to any of the freakish horrors of my life, so now I was going to exercise my freedom of choice and spend time with the river rats. Those rats were giant and scary. When you saw one, you knew you were someplace the CHUMS God did not intend for you to be.

I felt free, but look at where I had to go to claim my freedom. On warm days, the river smelled like sewer backup, and I would often get cuts and bruises from navigating the fences and foliage. Then, because I was addicted to skipping school and would do it almost everyday, I ran out of classmates to join me. The people who used to be my allies were now yelling at me to get myself together and to stop skipping so much. There were many days I would sit alone with the stench of the river and the shadows of the rats. This wasn't fun anymore, but I didn't know how to change it. So, my days were filled with the challenges of restaurant managers and river rats. These are the things that dreams are made of.

Protractor

When you read a story or see a movie that includes a shady or undesirable character, why is it that they often have beady little eyes? When you think back to real life, you find that shady characters do indeed have eyes like needles. Such was the case with my freshman drafting teacher. As fantastic as I was at pretending my way through school, there was no way to fake perspective. In fact, my perspective has always been somewhat foggy.

I sat down at the drafting table, laid out all of my supplies, and then sat blankly trying to figure out how to balance the drawing. I must have traveled back to fourth grade for a moment, because I felt I would turn my head and see Artist Boy sitting at the next table over with the most precise drawing you could ever imagine. I could do nothing but brush away eraser shavings and look like I was hard at work.

Mr. Needle Eyes watched over and, instead of offering assistance, muttered insults such as, "This is what happens when they let girls in my classroom." His disdain was oozing all over my creation, staining my future as a drafter. But this man took part in shaping my destiny of easy-to-fuck-over. The more I struggled, the more he brought me down. He did, however, have some positive comments. They had more to do with the structure of my body rather than the structure of my compositions.

I played him appropriately. Whenever I found myself at odds, my sexual prowess could carry me through. So the way I got through the first three sections of drafting was to wear low-cut, tight-fitting shirts and to pretend like Mr. Needle Eyes was someone that I could admire. I managed to squeak out a C and two Ds with Her help on my homework. As earlier stated, She loved anything that had to do with drawing. She took pride in my homework and thus got me through classes.

During my last semester of drafting, She stopped helping me. He was having a violent semester, and She was too busy with beatings and gunfire. So now I was going to fail the class and would have to repeat it over the summer. This was too hostile a fate, but I realized I'd need some good fortune to avoid it. I was typically unfortunate, so I spent my days merely wondering what would come next.

I could not have predicted the insanity of Mr. Needle Eyes' next move. We had just received our yearbooks, and, through a dare, I asked Mr. Needle Eyes to sign my book. Unfortunately he decided to sign on his picture—where I had written "*Oh no!*" He signed "*Oh yes*" and asked me to stay after class for a moment. Most certain that a flogging of some sort would take place, I waited while clutching my suddenly aching stomach.

Mr. Needle Eyes told me that I was going to fail drafting and asked if I had a plan. To this I shrugged and said I thought he could offer me something. Offer he did. He scribbled something on a piece of paper and warned me not to open it until after school; if I was willing to comply, my grade could most definitely go up.

I went straight to the bathroom and read.

"Meet me after class, yes or no?" and the idiot had signed his name. I realized how stupid Mr. Needle Eyes thought I was. He must have felt I was so desperate to pass that I would come in after hours and suck his needle dick. There was no way I would even shake his filthy hand, let alone give him head.

I now needed someone wiser than me who I could trust. The only adult at that time who even came close was my gym coach. He was a cool guy and seemed to understand that physical education and I would never find harmony. I respected him for this and also thought he resembled J. J. Walker, and I loved Good Times (especially the Janet Jackson episodes) so I brought him the note. He read it and became stone-faced. Mr. Dynomite asked me what I was going to do with the note. I suggested the principal might like to see it. Mr. Dynomite said I would ruin Mr. Needle Eyes' career—like I cared. Luckily, Mr. Dynomite realized how I probably felt, so he began to think of a new angle.

"What do you want in return for this note?" he asked.

Without wavering, I wanted an A in drafting and in gym. I figured I may as well go for the mother lode. When would something like this ever happen again? Well, considering the source, it would probably happen many more times in my life, but this time I seemed to be in control. This was a great feeling! Mr. Dynomite said he would meet with Mr. Needle Eyes and get back to me.

That semester I came home with As in drafting and in gym. She was beside herself and asked me how I could have possibly pulled it off. I told Her I had earned it. You couldn't argue with that explanation, so—at least for now—I had won. Mr. Needle Eyes never brought it up and stopped harassing me altogether.

Mr. Dynomite told me I would have to find a new way to get through my sophomore year. I began to consider my options.

School's Out

I was so tired of being fat. My pale thighs jutted out from my weak hips. Friction, friction, friction—that was my usual walking pattern. My disability, however, did not stop my band of sex-seekers from trying to make my hips move in a more seductive manner. It's funny how someone so awkward could make men plead for a few moments of intimacy. Is that what you call it? I think it was more like they saw me and somehow knew I had been trained to take it like a bitch.

If I had this much power being fat and awkward, then imagine what havoc I could wreak being thin and agile. Since I could not become prom queen, and my GPA was being determined by how fast I could run along the riverbanks, I acquired a new goal. I was going to become skinny.

As I recall, I didn't really like food. She always made these meals of meat and potatoes, which I would choked down just to keep the peace. My girth probably had more to do with my lack of activity than my love for the typical all-American meal.

It was the seventies—people had not yet succumb to the "let's get physical" craze—and I couldn't exactly ask my family for help with this endeavor. These people got a workout by dancing around the wet bar in the basement. One of the inhabitants of the Pleasant Place was active. I think she was a gym teacher. I think she was also a lesbian. She hung around with a lot of beefy girls named Sue. There were also a lot of Girl Scout trips.

One day, the Chitty Chitty Bang Bang Girl asked me to go swimming with her. I thought this would be the ticket to my slimming down. After all, she was so slim and perfect. Her ass sat beautifully on her shapely thighs, which were also accentuated by her heavenly hips. So, I agreed to a swimming lesson. As I was sitting on the edge of the pool trying to gain some courage to jump in, the Chitty Chitty Bang Bang Girl gave me a push and in I went. Only I didn't know how to swim, and there was nine feet of water between me and the bottom.

I can remember the sensation of the water pulling me in. I couldn't breath and I couldn't fight. It was like my life. He was like a strong current—foreboding and unstoppable. I decided this would be a good way to die. The last person to touch me had been my idol in the world of Bang Bang. I gave into it and just sank.

At that moment, I felt the hand of an angel on my back. It was the Chitty Chitty Bang Bang Girl coming down to save me. She struggled with my weight, but she was the kind who wouldn't let someone die on her, so she persisted until we reached the top. I grabbed onto the edge and began to smell the sweet aroma of chlorine. I figured I would die another day and thanked her for saving my life.

She hung onto that for a long time, and whenever we fought, she would remind me that she had saved me.

Now I would have to find a new diet plan. It started quite innocently enough with Her Dexitrim. I swallowed the dark maroon capsule with great intention. It stuck in the back of my throat and opened up. The powder burned. It tasted awful and sweet all at the same time.

Then I waited to not be hungry. I stood staring into the snack cabinet, waiting for the Oreos to not look good. All at once, the packages began melding together. Shoestrings, spam, and marshmallows became one blob of disgusting food in my mind's eye. It worked! I left the snack cabinet and went for a smoke. The stuff made me crave nicotine instead of food. I was blissfully high.

Dexitrim was easy to buy but expensive, so I began to help out around the beauty shop to earn some extra money. After a while, however, the stuff didn't do anything for me. AA told me about something called speed. He said it worked better and lasted longer. For a nominal fee of a blowjob, I could have some for my own.

I would have turned him down, but I was trimming down nicely. I had already shrunk three pants sizes and was beginning to see the new, hot me. So I sucked just like he liked it and got my drugs. That night I smoked cigarettes and watched TV until dawn. The next day, I ate only a can of cling peaches and was totally satisfied. Summer was almost over, and I was going to reappear thin and confident. AA got a lot of blowjobs over the next couple of weeks, and I got into a size four. I was actually excited to go to school.

When the first day of school arrived, one of the Younger Set and I got out the trusty pliers. The trick was this: one of us would lie on the bed and muscle the sides of the zipper together, and the other would yank up the zipper with the pliers. We all managed to wear size threes that fall. I looked in the mirror and was amazed at the reflection. With the black eyeliner circling my eyes and the size threes hugging my ass, I was beautiful. For the first time in my life, there was promise. I hadn't been this excited about school since the platform shoe day. Even though that had turned out bad, I wouldn't be held back. She commented on the tightness of my pants, and I happily got on the bus.

People freaked out. "Omigod, you're so skinny!" I was in heaven. That morning at McDonald's, a guy approached me. Turns out that he was a friend of AA. They attended the all-boys' Catholic school down the street from my school. AA had put a good word in for me. I knew this would cost me in nighttime favors during our next sleepover, but it was cool. This guy was serious about school and a future. I thought he was so smart and caring. He convinced me to not cut class, and he rewarded me with companionship.

What was *this*? He didn't ask to feel me up or anything. I was in love.

We went out for six wonderful months. I took the bus to his house. We would go to his room and make out but not much more. He respected me and didn't believe in frivolous sex. All good things must come to an end, however, and every time I cut classes, he would stop talking to me. His last kindness came in the form of a favor. I had managed to skip thirty days of school without getting caught. I went home each day expecting to be grounded forever. That day never came. The school never called home and They never asked about homework. I knew, however, my luck would soon run out.

It seemed my love of smoking and speed had caught up with me, and I developed a nasty case of bronchitis. She thought

I should stay home and go to the doctor. I pleaded to go to school. She was proud of my dedication but insisted. I knew this must be serious, because we didn't go to the doctor for anything. I had broken my ankle in a skateboarding accident, and even though the ankle had swelled to four times its normal size, They'd refused to take me to the doctor. I now have bone fragments studding the ligaments of my right ankle.

I grudgingly went to the doctor. I was freaking out, because I knew my drug use would probably be apparent to a medical professional. However, I managed to dupe him as well. And as he left the room to consult with Her, I eyed the pad of doctor's notes. It hit me that this was my way out of my thirty-day truancy. I tore a few off of the top and shoved them in my pants. My heart was beating so fast. I was scared and exhilarated all at the same time.

The doctor came back in and wrote me a prescription for some cough medicine with codeine. I was about to get a new drug and a new lease on life. So the next day, I went to school high on cough medicine and toting a few stolen doctor's notes. I asked my love-boy to do me one last favor. He agreed but informed me that we were over. He could not be associated with someone bent on a path of self-destruction. I told him what to write:

Please excuse Kathleen for being absent from 2-25 to 3-25 due to a bout of pneumonia. She is now free of symptoms but should not participate in gym for another four weeks.

This was brilliant. I happily walked back into the building that I had been away from for so long. I had no idea what was going on in my classes, but the teachers were all so sympathetic, especially when I told them I had almost died from the disease. They all felt bad they hadn't known, because it was customary to send greetings from staff and students. Each teacher gave sincere apologies, offered to help me catch up, and signed off on the forged document. I was so pleased with myself. I was indeed a mastermind at beating the system. It seemed I had learned a few valuable lessons from Him. I had His talent. He would have been so proud, if only He knew…

Seventh period came. This had been a great day! I strutted into study hall with a new lease. I was going to attend school every day, catch up on my work, get my love-boy back, and smoke some pot. I handed the note to Mr. Hambone. It was now wrinkled, warm, and littered with signatures. Hambone took one look at it, tossed it back at me, and told me to go the office and get a reinstatement. This was standard procedure when a student had been out for more than three days. I had been out for thirty, however, and told him the office had given permission for this special circumstance. He then called the office and said I would be on my way. Now, I'd thought sourly, when I ended up dead from a drug overdose rather than becoming valedictorian, Hambone would be to blame.

There was quite a scene in the office that afternoon. First, they had to figure out how I had managed to be missing for so long without anyone taking notice. In short, they had screwed up and I was going to be made an example of so no one else would ever beat the system—and probably so they wouldn't have to enter into a liability suit. So much for their iron-clad attendance policy, and so much for my fresh academic start. I know that I was at fault for not attending school, but someone should have noticed. No one did, however, and now my parents were going to have to figure out what to do with me. Not a very promising situation because They hadn't known what to do with me from the start.

She was distraught. He seemed elated in saying I'd gotten kicked out of school in a big way. Now I was out of the honors

66

school and into the local high school. I suppose this was a better fit for me after all. The place was crawling with truants, sexual deviants, and drug peddlers. I began thinking about Johnny Sweetface and the crowd from elementary school. Maybe now they would be truly impressed with me—thin from drug use and snuggling up to social misfits.

It didn't take long for me to work around my new school schedule. The beautiful thing about this new academic haven was that they didn't even pretend to keep track of students—in or out of school. After looking at my new schedule, I decided to not stress myself too much and only went to morning class-es. Anyway, gym class was in the afternoon, and there was no way that I was going to get into the poofy, blue gym uniform. I was way too cool for that.

I spent my afternoons in the hangout across the street from the school. My fondest memory of this place was that they had Billy Thorpe's "Children of the Sun" on the jukebox. I used my lunch money to buy drugs and play that song over and over again.

I met some new people as well. There was this big, bad chick named Moe. Actually, she is now the third person I'll refer to by a real name. I could not nickname this chick any better. I guess her parents knew what they were doing.

One guy walked around with chains hanging from his waist and a gun sticking out of his pants. This little crew was responsible for 90 percent of the drugs going around school. I had no business associating with this group. I was bad but more of a naïve bad. Trouble called on me, and I answered out of fear that it would throw me against a wall. I had learned this from Her. Teach your children well.

At any rate, I was a good client for them. I spent my lunch money on pot, speed, or the drug of the day. They turned me onto all sorts of downers, LSD, and just about anything else to alter my reality.

After a while, I think they even began to like me. It seemed like they were going to bring me in. This meant status and cheaper drugs. As an initiation, Moe gave me twelve hits of acid. I could sell them for whatever I wanted, but I had to pay back the band $2.50 apiece.

This was so exciting for me. It was kind of like those perfume sets you could send away for. They would send you a little display case with twenty bottles of perfume knockoffs. When someone bought one, they would get to lift a tab on a page and see if they had won the bonus prize. I sent away for the set and would joyfully sniff all of the bottles. I would also get a bonus prize for selling the samples. She got a few of the beauty shop ladies to buy some and the Keeper of the Pleasant Place bought a couple samples. She was proud of my venture and gave me money to buy some as well.

The thing was, I wanted to open all of the tabs and see which one had the bonus prize, so I never told my customers about it. I was very careful, however, not to open tabs unless I had sold a sample. Eventually, I couldn't stand waiting and there was no way I was going to sell the last ten samples, so one night I smoked a lot of cigarettes, downed a pint of peppermint schnapps, and opened all of the tabs. I was so happy when I won the bonus. Now I would get two beautiful perfume sets of my very own. The problem was, now I had to come up with the rest of the money. One night, while He was passed out on the couch, I looked in His wallet and found a huge stack of twenties. I slipped one out and my problems were solved. She, however, would not let me send away for any more kits, stating I couldn't bother Her customers anymore.

Well, the drug sale sort of went like that. Every time I sold a hit, I carefully tucked the money away. I would add it up every night just to make sure it was still there. I only had two more hits to sell, and I wanted to give Moe the money the next day. It was like the perfume, I couldn't wait for the payoff. They would be so proud of me that they would make me one of them, and I would be cool and protected forever. I scraped together the money for the hits and let the tabs dissolve in my mouth. As I lay back and waited for the trip to begin, I thought of the perfume tabs and saw a future. Then, I spent the next twelve hours seeing the effects of the acid. I always hated to trip because you couldn't stop it no matter what you did. At least you could tame a pot buzz by eating.

I came down hard that morning, slept two hours, and then had to get up to go to school. My body was in bad shape. I was so weak and dizzy. I was still seeing things that weren't there, but I had purpose. That purpose dragged me on the bus and off to my learning institution.

I didn't even bother going to my morning classes that day. I had more important things to do. Becoming an honorary drug dealer was far more attractive than a lecture on World War II.

I sat down and waited for one of them to come in. I played "Children of the Sun" a few times and had a diet soda. Finally, at eleven o'clock, my new family walked through the door. I jumped up before the last one crossed the threshold. Moe didn't even acknowledge me. I followed them to the counter and just stood there. One of the guys finally turned around and asked me what the fuck I wanted. He said that he was in the mood to stick his dick in someone's mouth, but I said I had a sore throat from dropping acid. Upon hearing this, Moe turned and asked me if I was taking her drugs. I said I had, but that I had paid for them. I explained that I had been too impatient to wait, and I was excited about delivering the cash to her. We went into the bathroom and I gave her the money. She praised my dedication and said she would talk to the guys about bringing me on. I pranced back to my seat and waited for an approach.

The group left and only Moe returned about twenty minutes later. I thought she was coming with good news, but she looked upset. My stomach started to churn. I could feel something bad about to happen. She said I should come out to the alley. I kept asking her what was wrong, but she wouldn't even answer. I was so scared that I said I had to get home and I would catch up with them tomorrow. She told me if I knew what was good for me, I would just go along.

Once in the alley, she started yelling like crazy and the guys made a circle around me. Moe said I hadn't given them enough money. I was short for two hits. "*The two hits you dropped!*"

I was shaking but insisted I had counted the money at least twenty times and that I had paid for everything. I was told to bring the five dollars the next day and then to never even look their way again. She kicked me to the ground. I got up and ran to the bus. I cried all of the way home. An old lady on the bus asked what was wrong, but I just shook my head. I wanted to purge, but who would really understand this nightmare that was my life?

Well, now I had to come up with another five dollars and I was flat broke. His wallet was empty and She would only give me two dollars for lunch. I found another two in the piggy banks of the Younger Set and went through my pockets for another buck in change. I didn't sleep at all that night. I knew I was in trouble, big-time. This would not just go away. I sensed this whole thing was going to be life-changing. Maybe they would kill me. That would certainly be life-changing. I thought about not going to school the next day, but I knew that would stir up more trouble. So, I stuffed the money in my pocket and got on the bus.

I didn't go to school for my morning classes again. As I sat, I was wondering why no one had called to see why I hadn't shown up for class. Maybe they thought I had changed my mind or something. Or perhaps that I had suffered an untimely death at the hands of a drug dealer named Moe. Of course, no one really noticed that this whole gang never went to school, either. These random thoughts were keeping me together as I awaited my doom.

The door opened and one of the group's flunkies came to collect the money. I handed it over. Could this be it? Was I going to be saved? Did they really just want their money? As I sat there asking myself really stupid questions, the door reopened. The flunky said I should come back to the alley.

Oh *shit*. Here was doom again. Me and doom were pretty good friends. After so many encounters, this feeling of forthcoming harm was familiar. I simply went into doom-mode and went back to the alley.

Moe grabbed me and threw me into a brick wall. It didn't really hurt too much, but I cried anyway. If they thought they were really punishing me, then perhaps they would end the whole scene a lot sooner. I told her she had her money, and so there was no reason to kick my ass. Then Moe imparted some drug dealer wisdom on me that I never forgot. I still don't see the logic, but it's fresh in my mind.

Moe explained that by giving them the money, I had proven myself guilty. This prompted me to ask what would have happened if I hadn't brought the money. Moe explained I would still have been in for an ass-kicking, but maybe not as severe, since I'd had the guts to stand up to them.

Now that would be the day: when I stood up to those I feared. I was afraid of most people. He had seen to that.

So the group proceeded to beat me bloody—a kick to the face, a punch in the stomach, and then a face-slamming against a parking barrier. I got up and ran to the bus. They pulled me off and started the process all over again. When the next bus came, they let me get on. I dragged myself into the house. She completely freaked out. I was quite a sight, bleeding from most areas of my body. She wanted to call the police, but when I told Her the whole story, we decided to leave well enough alone. We would, however, have to go to the school and file a report. When He got home from work that night, He commented on my beautiful appearance and said He could have done a much better job redecorating my face. Then He asked His favorite question: "Does your face hurt?" His chuckles pinched at any feeling left in my being. "Well, it's sure killing me!"

Could You Hold onto This for Me?

Just getting over the shock that I'd skipped school for a whole month, They now had to deal with the fact that I had never signed in to my afternoon classes and that I would have to be escorted to school for protection from my fellow drug dealers. He suggested I just let them get me; eventually, I would learn my lesson. She was just plain tired of my treacherous academic career. It seemed the only thing I had learned in school so far was that I was puny and weak, that people would continue to fuck me over because of this, that the establishment was only concerned with getting through the day and not overly worried about how many kids get lost in the process, and that it's easier to just quit rather than fight.

All of this was reinforced on that day. The solution? I should quit high school and go to beauty school.

Because I was not sixteen, we would have to work with a social service agency to make it work. The school suggested that we see the Worker on Site. This was the person who had hung out with us at the restaurant across the street from the school. The goal of the Worker on Site was to connect with the students and encourage us to "achieve and believe." Because I spent so much time in the restaurant, I got to know the Worker pretty well. The Worker got to know me as well and seemed interested in me and my story. We had endless conversations about the people who had spewed me into this world and about the spew I had been swimming in ever since.

Even though this guy was hired by the establishment, he didn't seem to believe their false promises either. In essence, the Worker was one of us—just a little older with curly hair and a mustache. He was sort of like Gabe Kaplan in *Welcome Back, Kotter* and I was sort of like Debralee Scott. Well, at least that's who I wanted to be. She was my favorite Sweathog, and I thought she was so hot. I did my hair like her and wore those signature, tight pants. Like Mr. Kotter, the Worker didn't see us as rebels but as results of bad parenting and horrible schooling.

The high school would contact the Worker and get the ball rolling. That was it! I was free! From my kindergarten keel to my drug dealer deluge, the nightmare was finally over. I somehow knew that being on my own would be far better. I could go back to school later. She really wanted me to go to beauty school, but I just wanted to get a job. I wanted nothing to do with school for a long time.

The very next week, I went with Them to the Outreach Center. I could tell He hated it, because He would get especially drunk before we left. I, on the other hand, liked having someone care about me. The Worker took the time to know me and attempted to repair the structure of the family. You can't call the local plumber, however, when a dam breaks. You need an engineer. Eventually, They didn't want to go to the center, so I began going on my own. This was better anyway. I couldn't stand to be in the car with Him when He was drinking. He would drive too fast, get in fights with other drivers, and yell at whoever was in the car with Him.

The Worker and I had a good relationship. It was honest and caring. Almost loving. No one had ever cared about me before, so why not become mesmerized with the person that could turn me around? This is what I most admired about the Worker—that he was going to save me. Kind of like how the Chitty Chitty Bang Bang Girl had when I was drowning. My lifestyle would eventually kill me, like being under water too long. The Worker was strong enough to keep me afloat.

And then came the bad news. My savior needed knee surgery and would not be able to meet with me for at least four months. There were consultations, the surgery, physical therapy, and time for healing to consider. He was going to take a leave of absence, so we could not technically see each other.

I was devastated. I asked if there was any way for us to keep in touch. The Worker gave me his number and said it would be okay if I visited him in the hospital. I promised I would and took leave of my lifeline.

I managed to wait for two weeks without calling. Finally, I couldn't stand it anymore and I called. My heart was beating so fast. Why was I so nervous? Calling the Worker at home was changing the dynamic of the relationship, and there was also the fear that I would lose this guy just like the CHUMS God. The Worker answered and relayed that he was to have surgery that weekend. He said I could visit him the week after. I wrote down the directions to the hospital and wished him well.

There was no way I could do this by myself, so I paid this girl I knew with drugs to come with me. I had many more of these types of friends now. They were people that would hang out with me as long as they were getting something out of it. I didn't mind too much, because at least I was not alone all of the time. On the hospital-visiting day, I walked over to her house. We smoked some pot on the way to the hospital in between bus rides. I'm not sure how far this place was, but it took us about two hours to get there. I was glad to have help and a buzz buddy. When we approached the hospital, however, my buzz vanished and my heart was racing again. It wasn't the same as doom–mode, but it was sort of a combination of schoolgirl excitement bundled with a dose of normal anxiety. Kind of like mixing speed with schnapps. It's funny that I could process this feeling artificially, but when it was happening for real, it was alien. Twenty-five years later, real feelings are still a mystery. I know it's okay to feel something, but it still seems artificial.

My paid escort and I went up to the nurses' station and asked to see the Worker. First of all, we did not know his last name. I guess it never came up. Secondly, we were told that we were not family and that the surgery had been pretty brutal—the patient really shouldn't have visitors. All of a sudden, I changed into someone with conviction. No one, after all, was going to keep me from my Worker.

I explained that we had traveled two hours by bus and that she at least had to ask the patient if he wanted visitors or not. I had been in enough treatment centers and hospitals with Him during the several times He had tried to dry out—I sort of knew how these places worked. So, I told the nurse that patients have rights and that my Worker patient had the right to know we were there.

Five minutes later, we were on our way to see my beloved Worker. I don't think, however, I was prepared for what I was going to see. This guy was in bad shape. Tubes, wires, and slings were attached so many places that he didn't even look human. I told my escort that the scene was ruining my buzz. She agreed.

I carefully stepped over to the bed and began to cry. For a moment the Worker reminded me of Him after a bottle of Canadian Club. This was too much for me to bear. I really did love this man for helping to make me feel whole again, and now he looked barely alive. The Worker looked up at me and said my eyeliner was running. That was his way of cheering me up, and I laughed. I then introduced him to my escort and told him how long it took to get there and how high we got in between buses. The Worker said he was glad that we'd come, because he had no family. I was the only one who would be stopping by.

This made me love him even more. We were both alone in the world. I would be his little girl and he could be my daddy. I just needed someone to make sense of it all. I so yearned for someone to hold me and make it all okay. I craved feeling safe and warm. My Worker, beaten and broken, appeared as an angel to me that day.

Then, the nurse came in and told me we would have to go. The Worker said he would be going home in a few days and asked if I could please come and see him. Of course I would. I would think of nothing else until that day came.

A few days later, my Worker left the hospital to heal at home. I would call every day to see how he was doing. I felt sad because he said it was hard for him to get around and he didn't have anyone to help him. I assured him I would be helpful when I arrived. We set the date for two days later. I had another long bus ride in store, but I couldn't wait to spend time talking and laughing with my angel Worker.

I struggled with the question of bringing my escort or going alone. I eventually decided to go this one solo. Anyway, I knew she would just smoke all of my pot, and I was hoping I could smoke some with the Worker. We had never done this before, but he'd told me he liked to do it occasionally. I rolled a joint with love, grabbed a few dollars out of His wallet, and got on the road. I had that weird speed/schnapps feeling again.

When I arrived at the apartment, the door was open and I let myself in. The Worker was lying in bed, looking busted up by life. I knew how this felt so automatically, I felt his pain. I asked him what I could do. The place was a mess. Carry out food boxes and drink containers littered the place. He asked if I wouldn't mind cleaning up. I had experience with this type of thing. My first job at the age of ten was cleaning for an old woman down the street, and of course I had many chores to do at home. She worked and He drank. That left the Younger Set and me to maintain the house.

I set off to work. It felt so good to be helping the Worker. He then asked if I wouldn't mind cleaning the bathroom. I got down on the floor and began wiping behind the toilet. It was so disgusting I thought I would be sick, but I was still high on the speed/schnapps feeling, so I kept going.

The Worker then told me that I was going to be rewarded for my good deeds. He pulled out the biggest bag of weed I would ever see in my long drug life. The Worker rolled a beautiful, round joint. He talked to me while he was doing it. He explained that if the roll wasn't performed correctly, it could ruin the whole experience. After that day, I always rolled my joints like the Worker. We smoked and talked about his pain, my pain, and how deeply we felt connected. Then he began to perform an interview of sorts.

"So Kathleen, do you have a boyfriend?" He asked. I told him that many guys were interested in me but really only wanted one thing. The Worker was very interested in this. "But you're so beautiful. That's why they want you. You must be the most beautiful girl that I've ever seen."

Well, I was high from really good, adult Worker drugs and from really good, adult Worker charm. He then asked what I did with guys. This made me quite shy. Should I tell him about AA? Johnny Sweetface? I just couldn't. This guy was my idol. He couldn't know about all of the horribly slutty things I had done. I felt really ashamed. The Worker told me it was okay, because a lot of girls experience sex early in life and that it actually makes them stronger women. He then asked me if I could help him to the bathroom. I lifted him with all my strength, and when he leaned his weight into me, I thought I might die from happiness.

The Worker told me he hadn't taken a shower since arriving home from the hospital because he was afraid of falling with no one around. I told him I had time, and a shower would make him feel better. While listening to the water run, I lay in his bed and inhaled the sweet aroma of Worker scents. Looking back, it wasn't really that sweet. There was a strange mix of old perspiration, hospital, pot smoke, and dirty penis. As I mentioned before, however, I took what was available to me and drifted off to sleep.

When I woke up, the Worker was standing above me in a terry cloth skirt. I had seen these before. I even think He had one. It was sort of repulsive to see my lovely Worker in the garment.

"Can I lay down with you?" He asked. I was a little uncertain, but of course I agreed. "Have you ever seen one of these before?" He asked.

I told the Worker that He had one, but it was blue. Confusion came over the Worker's face.

"Oh, not the bath wrap," he said—and pointed to his erection. I, in fact, had seen way too many of these, and I certainly was not interested in seeing his. But I went along just like I'd been taught. I told him I had seen and felt many, but it was usually under some kind of force and that I really didn't want to think of him in that way.

"You want to help me feel better? Right?" he asked.

I did, so much, want to help him, so I began to do what he wanted. But all I could do was cry. I kept on crying, and he kept on pushing his hard-on into my hand. I asked him to please understand that I could not do this for him, but his skirt was open and his ears were closed.

All at once, I got up and ran, but not without slipping his bag of great, adult Worker weed into my pocket. I had to feel victorious somehow.

I didn't feel like a champion, however. I felt like a whore. No one would ever want me for anything else. Maybe that's why the CHUMS God betrayed me. I figured even he would have wanted me to give him a hand job.

Barbershop Guy

After a brief job hunt, I managed to find full-time employment at a local department store. I lied about my age and started at $3.10 per hour. This was less than I had made cleaning houses, and far less than dealing drugs, but I had benefits. I also had independence, freedom, and endless cigarette money. I vowed to stop taking money out of His wallet. I had also been taking His Valium. All the stress of the beating and losing my Worker had gotten the best of me. I could not eat, spent most of my daytime hours in the bathroom, and was smoking close to two packs a day. The payoff, though, was that I had this new, hot body that drove men crazy.

It was a different kind of crazy than when I was fat and frivolous. Now, I had this tiny little waist that accentuated my round ass. My clothing size was a comfortable three. I had long, flowing, almost-black hair and wore heavy, black eyeliner around my deep, brown eyes. I had difficulty walking down the street. Literally, every two feet, someone would be yelling from a car window or leering my way as I passed by. I loved this. After all of my years of ugliness, I was a swan and the predators were flocking to be near me.

I got pretty used to the routine of walking to work under the deluge of catcalls. The most interesting, however, came from the guy who owned the barbershop I passed on the way. If he was busy cutting hair, he would stop and wave. If he was on the phone, he would drop the phone and come out to say hello. Since I came by at the same time everyday, Barbershop Guy would usually be standing in the doorway to greet me. Mostly, I was flattered to have the attention. We would exchange pleasantries and I would be on my way.

The barbershop closed early, so on my walk home I did not see the Barbershop Guy. That was okay with me, because I sometimes got tired of talking to him. He was always there, and it sometimes seemed like he was waiting for me when I came past. This started to creep me out a little.

I found an alternative path to work that avoided the barbershop, and some days I would bypass the shop just to get a little relief. On one of those days, I was passing by on my way home, and to my surprise, the Barbershop Guy was waiting at his doorway for me.

He asked where I had been. I made up a quick excuse that She had just got Her driver's license and that She had been driving me for practice. The Barbershop Guy told me he had missed me and that he had a friend who he wanted me to meet. I was completely apprehensive, but in these situations I tended to do exactly the opposite of what I wanted to do; I went in to meet the friend.

Barbershop Guy introduced me to his friend, the Modeling Agent. He told me he had been talking me up to the Agent and that I had a very good chance of becoming famous. I pondered this for a moment and asked what agency the friend was from. They both mumbled something completely different and then saved the blunder with a pitch.

The pitch was that there were several high-profile gentlemen they were associated with who were in need of beautiful escorts. The escort's job was to join these dignitaries on trips and meetings. In return, a modeling contract would be awarded for excellence in service. On top of the modeling contract, I would be paid a hundred dollars per hour of service.

I had learned a great deal of things during my tenure of taboo, but had not had much experience with being a model/escort. I had to think, but they kept talking. The Agent was critiquing my body and the Barbershop Guy was expressing everything that had kept him watching me over the past few months.

I was dizzy. I first thought about the fact that the only thing I had put into my body that day was three-fourths of a pack of Newports. Secondly, I thought about the possibilities of all of that money. Obviously, my initial thought was endless drugs, but then my mind turned to getting out of the madhouse. That kind of money could buy drugs and pay rent. If I'd thought breaking away from my academic noose was liberating, then this would be absolutely cathartic.

"Kathleen, Kathleen."

Shit! Why were they calling me that? It was ruining my hungry buzz. Anyway, the insignia snapped me back to reality. These guys were talking about prostitution. Did I want to be a whore? This was a good question, seeing how I'd already been one since the tender age of eleven. Wasn't that the definition of the word? Guys do things to you and you let them. Sometimes they give you drugs, sometimes they give you friendship, and sometimes they give you money. But sometimes they don't give you anything except more whore experiences.

I was wondering what that was called when the Agent told me to come closer to him. I was wearing a tube top that day. I didn't wear them too often because I have linebacker shoulders—they look good in a tank top, but definitely not in a tube top—but that was all I'd had clean to wear that day.

I walked up to the Agent and I thought he was going to shake my hand, but instead he pulled my top down to my waist. So there I was, in the barbershop with my chest exposed with two old dudes sizing me up for service. The Agent grabbed a hold of my tender young breast and told me I needed some firming. Then the Barbershop Guy grabbed onto the other one and began a rebuttal based on the fact that my skin was a perfect ivory color and that I was so young and tantalizing. Both of the men let go of me and I started to pull up my top. I was stopped, however, by the agent. He said he needed to see all of me before the deal could go through. I was asked to unbutton my pants and to strip down to my underwear.

For a second my only thought was if I was wearing any or not, and if I was, what did they look like? It's funny that I would be concerned with such trivial matters when I was standing in the back of a barbershop, topless, determining my future as a teenage whore. Would I graduate to porn, I wondered?

The Agent went right for the button on my jeans. He struggled with the tightness of the pants. I began to explain about how we zipped them up with pliers, but the Agent told me to just get them down. Because my pants were so tight, my underwear came down with them. The Agent was so excited by my audacity that he told the Barbershop Guy I was the right girl for the job. I was actually feeling highly embarrassed and just wanted to get the hell out of there.

I told the Agent that I had to get going. He asked me to wait about five more minutes so we could work out the details. I was asked to turn around, and when those guys saw the beautiful and round sixteen-year-old ass before them, they became speechless. The Agent grabbed at it and the Barbershop Guy rubbed gently. Then, the Barbershop Guy started to reach between my legs. This was way too much for me, and I insisted that She would be looking for me, and since I'd disappeared before, She would call the police if I wasn't home on time.

The two men shuddered at the idea of the police being called and told me to get dressed. The agent told me I had a good fifteen pounds to lose before I would be considered for modeling. I thought this notion was crazy. I was already rail thin, and dropping to a hundred pounds, for me, would have been detrimental. The Agent told me I could still do the escort version of the job while I was getting in shape, and then I would have enough money to pay for pictures. I told the men I would have to think about all of this and that I would get back to them in a few days.

When I got home, I thought a lot about the day. I was slightly sickened by the scene, but was also a little turned on. It was the idea of all of that money and of breaking free that was making my blood pump with anticipation.

Later on AA came over so I could buy him some beer from the local liquor store. I had gone in there so much with Him that the guys thought I was old enough to buy beer. While we walked back I told AA about my afternoon and showed him the business card the Agent had given me. AA was a little concerned about the whole prospect and told me it sounded like something I shouldn't get involved with. He also suggested I talk with an adult.

I thought this was crazy. Who could I ask about whether or not I should become a whore? AA then began to ask me details of the event and wanted to know if I would let him be the judge of the whole weight issue. I wasn't in the mood for his advances, so I told him he should take his beer and go home.

I decided that night not to go on tour with the Agent and the Barbershop Guy. I wanted the money, but I remembered being scared the whole time I was in there with them. I was already living with enough fear and didn't want to add to my case load. I avoided the barbershop for the next three weeks, both to and from work. One day I had to walk past, however, with my manager on the way to make a bank deposit. It was customary for the store manager or assistant manager to make the bank deposit with another employee for the sake of accountability. So, on that day we were walking past, and as soon as the Barbershop Guy saw me, he dropped his scissors and ran to the door. Oh, how I hoped he wouldn't inquire about my short-lived prostitution career. He simply asked me where I had been and if I was okay. I introduced him to my manager, who, of course, he already knew since the Manager walked by each day. I said I had been fine, but I had found a better route to work. We left it at that and said goodbye.

As we walked, I told the Manager that the Barbershop Guy had begun to creep me out so that was why I had changed my walking route. The Manager told me he had heard that the guy had mob ties and that I should stay far away from him. This time, fear worked for me and led me to safety rather than to pain and uncertainty.

The Banker

Your button is open." I'm in the bank with the store manager making the daily deposit and The Banker opens right up to let me know I'm hanging out of my shirt. At that moment, he also passed me a piece of paper with his phone number on it. My manager asked if I was going to call him. It occurred to me that the ball was in my court. I was not usually the one in the power seat, but this time I was and it felt great. I decided to take it slow and not call right away.

So the next day, I wore a low-cut shirt and a tight pair of dress slacks to work. I did this so I could make my Banker sweat a little and guarantee my power position for a while longer. Anyway, the District Managers were in the store that day and they loved it when I dressed that way.

I'm not sure if workplace sex was more accepted in the eighties or if DMs were just hornier, but whatever the case, these guys were not shy about what they were thinking. One had come right up to me and said I must be trying to kill him, because I looked so good in my pants that his heart was going to burst. Now that I think about it, he could have been much more forward and spoken of another organ swelling with blood. Then the guys would get together in the next aisle and talk about my ass. They did it in the same tone they used while speaking about profit and loss. In fact, one would be talking about a new inventory procedure and the other would answer the inquiry with a comment about how good I must look naked.

This idea had prompted the men to ask me to help out with inventory. I would have to work through the night on two different occasions. They'd even asked me to wear something slutty. I'd just laughed. This really was the eighties. I'd shown up for inventory in a new pair of tight jeans the Younger Set had had to help me get on with the aid of the trusty pliers. I'd also purposely left my bra at home. Every time I'd bent down to count an item on the bottom shelf, all eyes had been on me. I'd been sure this would get me a promotion of some type.

The point of all of this is that I knew this outfit would make the Banker wait breathlessly for my call.

The initial conversation wasn't very exciting, but we agreed to go out the following Friday. It was only Tuesday, and I didn't know how I was going to wait that long. I was pretty excited. Even though I had fucked a great many boys and men, I had never gone out on a real date. I couldn't even imagine what this was going to be like. Imagine I did, however, for the next three days. I wondered if the Banker would open doors for me. Would he buy me dinner, a movie? I hoped he would put his arm around me just like in the movies and lightly touch my breast. That would be so romantic.

Then, the other side of me chimed in. This was the girl who had been fucked around by every person she had ever trusted or cared about. This girl imagined the Banker tying her up with his Banker tie and raping her repeatedly. She wondered if he would get a blow job in the back seat or the front seat of his car. And she also suspected that he would bring a friend along to bang her as well in payment for some past debt.

These two girls, Hopeful and Hopeless, were at war. It was kind of like the movie *Sybil.* There were these two very different personalities that would come out depending on the circumstance. I know Sybil had, like, sixteen of these personalities, but I figured that I was well on my way. I could be the scared little girl, the sexy seductress, the cunning thief, the protector of the Younger Set, and the keeper of all things fucked up. Well, that was already like five or six, so if I kept working at it, I could possibly work up to at least twelve.

This little personality problem worked to get me through to Thursday evening. The Banker called to set plans. He would pick me up at 7:30 and we would go to dinner. He asked me what type of food I liked.

This was a curious question. I didn't really know. I had always eaten what was placed in front of me—I think I already chronicled the menus of SPAM and smoked butt. I realized I had no personality. This is a strange realization for someone who, just hours ago, thought she had twelve.

I think that was Sybil's problem. She had no real personality of her own. The abuse and associated trauma had destroyed any real personality she might have developed. The result was a morphing of all of the responses she had ever had to the abuse.

Wow! Who the hell needs Dr. Wilbur? Did she ever really evaluate the situation, or did she just purvey some psychobabble and then reap the rewards of the disappearing personalities? Whatever the case, I now had to figure out what kind of food I liked in the next five seconds so I wouldn't sound lame.

The Banker was calling my name, and I came back to the present situation. I thought quickly. I was Italian, so I must like Italian food. That was my request. Perfect! We would go out for spaghetti.

I shopped around at work for something to wear that would ensure my Banker would come back for more. I looked at the pretty dresses, but the nightmare of my eighth grade graduation dress pushed me to the casual clothing department. I settled on a pair of jeans with stitching on the pockets and a button-down shirt. I felt this was appropriate.

I rushed home and changed. I was ready by 6:30, so I decided to wait on the front porch for prince charming to show up. The Younger Set were teasing me about going on a date and She quizzed me about where we would go. He, on the other hand, gave me His famous advice to keep my legs crossed. While I was waiting I smoked eight cigarettes. Now I would smell really bad, so I rushed in to brush my teeth.

While I was trying to kill the nicotine breath, the bell rang. Oh Shit! I did not want the Banker to come into this fortress of doom. That would definitely be the deal breaker. I ran to the door and yelled goodbye.

Whew! I was safe. I said a cheerful hello to the Banker and said let's go. He asked if my parents needed to meet him and I told him They didn't really exist, so it wasn't really an issue. The Banker seemed confused, but said he was happy I was going out with him.

We walked to the car and he walked with me to my side and opened the door for me. I knew instantly he was going to get lucky that night. He informed me we were going to stay in the neighborhood and eat at this little place he liked to go to with people from work. When we got to the restaurant, he got out of the car and opened my door. I was in heaven. I was certain I was going to marry him and give him lots of children. Before we sat down, he pulled out my chair for me and touched my shoulder as I sat down. My Banker then told me to order whatever I wanted from the menu. He said it was my night. I looked over the menu but did not really know what half of the items were. He asked if I was okay. I then realized I had a huge look of fear on my face. It's funny how bullets flying and being asked what I wanted for dinner evoked the same response. I simply replied that I would have whatever he was having. This must have been the right thing to say, because he smiled and replied that he would take good care of me.

While we waited for the food to arrive, the Banker asked me about my job and if I was working my way through college. It occurred to me that he had no idea how old I was, and that I probably couldn't even spell college, let alone fill out an admission form. I wondered if I should lie or come clean. There was something about this guy that told me he would like me no matter what, so I came clean. I told him about Moe and about Mr. Needle Eyes. There was a look of shock combined with a look of excitement on his face. Then I told him I would be turning sixteen in a few weeks. The fact that he was twenty and I was jailbait spooked him a little, but he said something about me being worth the risk.

After dinner he took me home, kissed me goodnight, and said he wanted to see me again. No blowjob! I was somewhat taken back, and a little insulted that he didn't want to get in my pants, but there was no room for him in those jeans anyway, so I walked dreamily into the lair. I prayed to the CHUMS God that He would be sleeping. I didn't feel like dealing with His comments or a disruption of my inner peace. Incredible! I hadn't smoked anything, not even a cigarette, since I'd left the house, and I was high. These things were simply a substitute for love. I vowed to clean up a little for my Banker.

Escape

"Kathy!" She was screaming from the kitchen. I tried to get my head off of the pillow to see what time it was. I felt like I had just fallen asleep. It was still dark outside, so it couldn't be morning yet.

As I opened my eyes, I saw the Younger Set sitting by my bedside, also trying to get me to wake up. What the hell was going on? Her screams got more frantic. I followed protocol by giving the Younger Set the phone to call the police if things got out of hand, and I ran toward the screams.

As I'm writing this, I am thinking about how, over twenty-five years later, I am still jumpy. Even if one of my kids trips over their own feet, I run with the same urgency to see if everything is all right. Fear is one of those things that never really goes away completely. Small triggers continually bring on enormous responses.

So, I rushed to save the day just like Underdog. I loved that show. Underdog was my hero. He was always there whenever Polly was afraid. I wished Underdog were there now.

He was lying on the floor, bouncing up and down and shaking all over. I had never seen anything like it before. I was scared, but in a way I hoped He was dying. I imagined my life without Him, and I felt calm—except that She was screaming His name over and over again like that would stop the shaking. I yelled to the Younger Set to call an ambulance—not the police, for once.

I waited outside for the paramedics the same way I would wait for the police. By the time I let them into the house, He was already coming to. He didn't know where He was and who we were. This really was a dream come true. One of the paramedics said that He had bit his tongue deeply, and they would have to take Him to the hospital to see what was going on. She grabbed Her purse and told me to take care of the Younger Set, and I would get a call soon to hear what was going on.

I soon learned how to stick a butter knife in His mouth while He was seizing. His brain was so fried from booze and pills that He spent many nights like that. We stopped calling the hospital and began to celebrate when He had a seizure, because He would be calm for days after.

He rarely left the house now except to replenish Canadian Club and Kools. He also lost most of His bodily control. We would often come home to see Him sleeping in a pool of vomit or excrement. The couch acquired a plastic undercover overlaid with bath towels.

Thank CHUMS God for my Banker. I was seldom home to witness the chaos. Somewhere in my bliss, however, I forgot about the Younger Set and how they no longer had me to help them ride the storm out.

I think they were learning to lean on each other. She was working most of the time to keep up the bills and drinking the rest to help cope with the mass of flesh that covered the sofa. The only good thing about His cathartic state was that the violence was almost gone. He was so weak that no one was really afraid of Him anymore. I'm not sure of all that was going on in the house, because I was too involved in my Banker Bliss.

I taught him all of my ways of my world. The Banker smoked his first joint with me, downed pints of peppermint schnapps in the alley, and got his first blowjob in the back seat of his car. We got high every night and would pair food with our drug of choice. Those nights caused me to miss many days of work. Even the DMs had no use for me anymore, due to my growing waistline. Eventually I was fired and spent my days in the house waiting for my Banker to get off of work.

The downside to that was that I was stuck all day watching Him drinking Canadian Club. He would even enlist me to mix the drinks and make Him burgers. He told me about the voices in His head and how they would kill Him soon. He also told me that I was getting fat, and if I kept it up that no guy would want to stick it in me anymore. I guess that time was the closest I would ever come to bonding with Him, and I was used to settling for whatever insanity was placed in front of me and accepting it as the norm. I knew, however, that I had to get out of there. I was now smoking over two packs of cigarettes every day and was completely unavailable to the Younger Set and any other responsibility. I cried to the Banker every day about how bad it was and pleaded with him to help me get out.

One night, he picked me up and told me that he had a surprise for me. We hopped in the car and drove a couple of miles. As we turned down the side street, I recognized the neighborhood. This was where Her parents lived. I wondered how a visit to the grandparents would lift my spirits. Our destination, however, was across the street. We walked through the gangway and he put a key into the lock of the door. I asked who lived there and he said I did.

How could this be? I didn't have a job or any means to support myself, and here I was, standing in my apartment. My Banker bought me freedom. He explained that we were spending so much money on motels that this was a money-saving move. Now we could dress up and play our games at any time without having to sign in.

The only condition was that his mom couldn't know. She would cut him off if she knew we were living in sin. I guess I hoped my Banker would live with me, but it seemed I would have to play house alone.

The Keeper of the Pleasant Place gave me some old furniture and a TV. I got some old dishes from home, and I was all set. There was a live phone line in the place, and I only had to hang up when the owner would pick up to use the phone. I packed up my clothes and said my goodbyes to the nightmares of my past and to the Younger Set, who were now truly on their own. They pleaded with me not to go. Who would take care of them, see that they ate, were safe, and kiss them goodnight? I was their mom and I was leaving. I struggled with this, but I just couldn't be responsible for the wellbeing of this family anymore. And who was I kidding? Wellbeing did not exist in this place. This was my goal in caring for the Younger Set, but I could never save them from this life, and if I didn't get out, I would surely self-destruct. I had to hope that they would be okay. They had each other and that would have to be enough. I grabbed my smokes and told them they could visit.

As a show of appreciation, and as a housewarming gift, I tied the Banker to the kitchen table and dripped candle wax on his quivering body. We then drank a bottle of tequila and drifted off to sleep. He awoke in a panic at 2:00 a.m. and rushed home.

Suddenly I was alone, and I was terrified. I missed the hum of the hair dryers, the rush of sneaking past Him so that He wouldn't wake up and breathe His wrath on me, and I missed my old fear. That was a fear that was familiar, but this new fear of being alone with no soul, no backbone, and no identity was too much to bear.

I sat by the TV all night, just trying to get warm. Finally, at dawn, when the foreboding darkness subsided, I went to sleep. I awoke to my Banker coming through the door. It was 5:00 p.m. He asked if I had slept all day and was slightly appalled. I explained that I had had a rough night and put on the tears until he felt sorry for me and offered to buy me dinner.

Excuse Me but Isn't That Your Dad

Divorce. This is usually a word that sends children into a state of confusion and sadness. When She told us, however, that She was finally going to get rid of the Beast, the Younger Set and I were joyous. It was almost the best news we had ever heard. The best news has to wait until the final chapter. No peeking.

Her father had broken down and grudgingly given Her some money to get out of hell. This life was hell. If the beatings and bullets had not been bad enough, this man could no longer take care of Himself. He had not worked in over a year, had been through treatment three times without success, and now only slept, puked, and drank.

She knew that They were going to lose everything if She didn't make a move. There was also the issue of Her doing everything. She worked, paid bills, did all of the housework and childcare, and had to take care of Him as well. I think what had kept Her from leaving before was the fear of doing it all alone. Now She'd proven to Herself that it was possible, and there was no longer a reason to put up with the madness. Now seemed like the best time to make a move. I had been living on my own for about a year, and the Younger Set were both in high school.

The papers were filed and the house sold. He was happy, because the proceeds from the house would keep Him on the couch for at least a year. He got some old furniture from the Keeper of the Pleasant Place. In order to keep the Pleasant Place very pleasant, the Keeper continually bought new things, so there were plenty of hand-me-downs to go around.

He and the new/old furniture moved to a basement apartment in the old neighborhood—nothing like living through most of your life and ending up right where you started. This must have been too much for Him to bear, because He drank more heavily than ever and began to hallucinate. For some reason She gave him the cats, and one night He put them out because He believed someone had sent the felines to help carry out a plot to kidnap Him and take Him to an alien nation.

Wouldn't that have been just hysterical? All along, He was an alien and He was just trying to get home—like ET. It would also explain the bullet making and my own erratic behavior. Maybe I was half human and half alien. The real me and the spawn of the evil alien were at war, and the only way that I could get peace was for the alien part of me to die and take leave of my spirit.

I couldn't believe that the cats were gone. I had loved them, but He took away everything that I ever loved, so this should have come as no surprise. It was reminiscent of His famous gerbil-flushing and dog-throwing. Even members of the animal world suffered His torture. We had had three gerbils, and the baby got sick. So, She and Her mother took the tiny animal to the vet. A few dollars for a visit and a dose of medicine promised relief for the animal. He, however, got wind of the medical visit and decided to teach us all a lesson about wasting money and valuable resources. We were all forced to go into the bathroom and watch Him flush the baby gerbil down the toilet.

One would have to choose whether this, throwing a young puppy down two flights of stairs, or letting two cats free in the dead of winter would win the father of the year award. The only victory in the whole situation was that one of our old neighbors called to say that one of the cats was crying on our front porch. The cat had found its way home. By the time we got there, however, he was gone, along with our victory, but our celebrations were only temporary anyway. People who know me as an adult call this my "waiting for the other shoe to drop" philosophy. It's one that states that happiness will only bring sadness. If you get caught smiling, then someone you love will get thrown against a wall, or a helpless gerbil will get flushed.

So now that He was out of our daily routine and off of the family couch, we should have been able to breathe, to relax, to sigh, and to take to the trash all of the debris that had cluttered our existence thus far. But the Gerbil Flusher would see to it that we would not be free just yet.

One night, about ten o'clock, there was a knock at my door. The Banker was already gone, so I was apprehensive to open the door. It was the Keeper's Keeper. He'd been sent to tell me that there had been an accident, but that He was okay.

Damn it, why wouldn't this guy die? He'd been beaten bloody once and survived because He'd had an extra spleen—I was beginning to fall for the whole alien theory. Anyway, it seemed that He'd thought that the aliens had come to get Him by sending a hundred people into His apartment, along with a general—just in case He put up a fight. The only way that He could escape was to climb into His station wagon and drive it right into the apartment. Once the front wall was gone, all the people would have room to get out.

The next day, the Banker took me to survey the wreckage. I was sick to my stomach upon seeing the front of the apartment gone and the car on the front lawn. He would be held accountable for His actions, of course, but He didn't have anything—so basically, the landlord was screwed as well.

It became my job to go through the apartment and find anything of value. There wasn't much to go through—He hadn't had a housewarming party. I threw some stuff into a box and got out of there. I was still in shock from the scene and was afraid that the damage to the structure would cause the building to come crashing down on me. I always picture dying this way, with things crashing on top of me and smothering me until I take my last breath. Then it occurred to me that He had no place to go. He was in the psych ward right now, but soon He would be released into our care. I didn't visit Him this time. All of the other times He was in treatment, I was forced to go visit Him. While visiting, I would think that if I ever had a kid and they got into drugs, that I would take them to one of these places to scare the thrill right out of them. Everyone inside looked dead already. They smoked a lot and ate Hershey bars. Coffee was also a staple in the treatment center. It seemed that the addictions weren't being cured, just replaced with something else. I guess this is why He would relapse within weeks of being released. I didn't assume that this time would be any different. No one would stop Him from being crazy.

She took Him in just until He could get settled someplace else. This turned into a three-month-long commitment. She had to re-cover the couch and replace the guard that She'd finally been allowed to let down after twenty years of torture. The Younger Set, now older, had no patience for Her last act of kindness in His regard. They would not talk to either of Them and spent many nights out.

One night, He came after Her with the fire in His glossy eyes that was now merely the glowing ember of a dying match. One of the Younger Set was not about to cower in the corner, and she kicked Him across the room. She put all the power and anger built up from the years of nightmares He'd put her through behind that kick. The Younger Set then told Her that He had to leave, or they would move in with me.

She only had a small idea of what went on in my apartment, but it was a large enough picture to see that the Younger Set would perish. She also didn't want to be alone with Him. So, She called the police and had Him dragged out. He held out an arm, reaching out to Her for one more chance. It seemed, however, that His chances were finally used up.

We were filled with a sense of relief, but also a fear of the unknown. Where would He go? He had no friends, and even the Keeper of the Pleasant Place would not help Him anymore. We knew that His only hope at this point was a homeless shelter. I guess that we still held onto a small glimmer of hope that He would either die or be saved.

The next day the Younger Set ventured out to catch the bus for school. The usual group that waited for the bus there had already congregated, but they were standing at least ten yards from the bus stop. As the Younger Set approached, the group suggested that maybe they didn't want to get too close to the bus stop bench. They could see that someone was lying there and not moving. The Younger Set asked if there had been an accident. A close friend leaned in and said that a homeless guy was sleeping there. Another bystander looked up and asked, "Isn't that your dad?"

Upon closer inspection, the Younger Set realized that waiting for the bus in the morning would be just like taking another bullet.

Looks Like We Made It

The Younger Set could not deal with the sight of Him sleeping on the bus bench every morning. Unlike me, they both had promising academic careers, and they would stop at nothing to make it to school. After one week of being humiliated every day, they took matters into their own hands and called the police. The next day the bus bench was empty, and their sanctity was restored. No one heard from Him for months. In a way, we were glad to have peace. She was working and managing to build an income. There were no more explosions or sawed-off shotguns.

Then one day the phone rang. As She explained it, He had a new place to live and was sober. There was a strange twist: He was sober and in therapy. When the cops had picked Him up off of the bench, they'd taken Him to a halfway house. It was there that He was introduced to a social worker that would give Him a new start in life. Unlike my Worker, she hadn't asked for a hand job. He was blessed with the luck of the leprechauns.

The social worker also gave Him a gift. This was the diagnosis of manic depression. Incredibly, the diagnosis also came with a payoff. Because He was disabled from the illness, the government saw fit to award Him with years of disability payments. The bastard got a check for twenty-five thousand dollars. At this point in His sobriety He could have made a move of restitution, to make up for a small percentage of the overwhelming evil that we'd suffered at His hand. But instead, He went off the wagon and purchased cases of Kool cigarettes and Canadian Club. He had a small apartment that was also subsidized by the state. He called me occasionally when He needed something. He had lost His license years ago and couldn't drive. If there was an appointment that was not accommodated by a bus schedule then I was on call. I hated going to that place, but I felt an obligation.

Wait! After surviving a life of pain and abuse, I still felt obliged to care for the Beast? This was the same type of mentality that had led me to service anyone in any way that they wanted.

The Banker and I had parted due to his inexplicable adoration for his abusive mother, who told him constantly what a "fucking bastard" he was and how she should have had him aborted. I would sit in on these love fests, and the strange thing was that it didn't seem that bad to me. The problem, however, was that my Banker put his maternal need before my internal needs, and I just had to get out.

Now that I was back in the family home, I was the contact person whenever the Monster would call. The Younger Set would not go visit, not talk on the phone, and would certainly not be doing any favors. This was my job, and I was painfully aware of it. Even the Keeper of the Pleasant Place would call me to make sure that I was taking care of my "dad." Who? I couldn't stand that word. It signified someone who held all of the power and none of the responsibility. Until He, the Beast, the Monster, my *dad* was put to rest, I would not be able to form a vision of a father being anything else.

And as for Her, my mother? Even though there were feelings of animosity for the disservice She'd laid upon us for not leaving, I loved Her. She was strong, She was dedicated, and She loved Her babies. As an adult, it is this love that I shower onto my own children. This is a love that could have only come from my mom.

A year or so passed, and He ran out of restitution for His disease. I was called on a weekly basis to bring food and to bring comfort to the dying. At this time, I was heavy with child and heavy with a new lease on life—my new mate had gotten me into therapy, which had begun the treacherous task of exorcising my past.

The phone would ring one more time. It was the Keeper of the Pleasant Place. I had assumed that there were groceries to be bought or a car to remove from a living room. The call, however, had been one that I had waited for since He took away my Santa Clause, my CHUMS God, and my spirit.

The Keeper's keeper had been summoned to the dungeon of the subsidized rental. Someone had reported a stench seeping from the walls of the fortress. The Keeper's keeper had to identify the body, which had been rotting for a week. The task wasn't easy, since His face had disintegrated into the carpet where He'd been lying, facedown, for a full seven days.

The Keeper asked me what I wanted to do with Him, because I was the legal custodian now. My request was to let the state have their way. It was, after all, the state that had given Him the money to drink Himself into decay. Oh, but a Catholic burial would have to be performed—none of this talk of burning and be-riddance. The Younger Set, one now married and another betrothed, did not care to fight. So, the burial took place.

I can't remember whether She came or not. I don't see Her face there. Maybe it's because She was free and flying above the catastrophe. We're free, I whispered, and I looked to the sky and said thanks to the CHUMS God. Was I grateful that He was dead? Was I feeling lucky for dodging all of the bullets? Or did I see the brightness of the future? In a way, I was feeling victorious. All one needs to overcome is the drive to keep going over and under each obstacle. Whether it be climbing the stairs to the Pleasant Place or climbing down the banks of the river, I found hope. It was a twisted and unrecognizable hope, but at least I had something to hang on to.

Looking over to The Younger Set, another realization set in. We had each other, and somehow this bond was more powerful than the evil we'd been forced to swallow. We grasped hands, and the coffin dropped.

Epilogue

I was rather unaffected by the death of my father. I felt a sense of relief but not loss. I guess that the Keeper of the Pleasant Place did me a favor by insisting on the funeral. Seeing the casket in the ground helped me feel like I would finally be safe. He couldn't haunt me anymore—tucked away underneath the dirt. Getting rid of Him, however, was not quite that easy. There are days when my every move is made out of fear. In some aspects, this is positive. In others, it is debilitating.

In parenting my children, I think about how my actions affect them. This has made me an insightful and nurturing parent. From the moment my daughter was born, I never left her. The nurses in the hospital begged me to set her down so I could eat and shower. There was no way I would leave her alone, to feel scared, to feel abandoned, or to have any need unattended to. She never had to cry when she was hungry. I knew what she needed before she needed it. I took her to sing- ing classes, playgroups, and paid for an expensive, early-child- hood Montessori experience. When it came time for her to at- tend public school, I volunteered for everything, including lice checks. Eventually I ended up working at her school. The bond we share is indescribable. The result has been mostly favorable. She tells me everything about her life, and I have been able to grow up again through her. Bailey's smile shows me what it is like to be whole.

I repeated the process with my son. I almost lost him dur- ing childbirth and during the many illnesses he suffered as a baby. I learn from him as well, but I also teach him how to be a good man. We talk endlessly about the right ways to love and respect others. I was fortunate enough to work at his schools and to see him grow and learn. Logan has my sensitivity and great empathy for others.

Victims of abuse either break or repeat the cycle. My biggest fear is that my children will feel pain. Even common illnesses and simple cuts and bruises, which they can shrug off, cause me to overreact, wanting to take it away. I know more than most that some pain is essential to the growth process, but I associate even small amounts with the trauma I knew. My kids make fun of me for freaking out, but they will never wonder if I love them.

Another cycle that I had to break was being uneducated. How could I inspire my children to reach for success when I was a drop out? After the death of my father, I found the courage to take the GED test. Some years later, I entered college. My kids saw how hard I worked and they truly understand the impor- tance and value of an education. My college graduation, with them in the arena, was an immense celebration in my life.

After that I sought a degree in education. I vowed to make a difference in the lives of every student I served. I knew when they were sad, tired, excited, engaged, or bored. I would not ignore a child because I feared what might be under the surface. I wish just one teacher would have reached out to me in school. It may have made a difference. I can say this from later experience during my college career. One professor saw through my tough, brooding exterior and reached out to me. The giant wall that I had built around myself intimidated all of the others. This professor got me through the toughest times in school, and now in my personal life.

People ask me why I wrote this book. In a sense, I want to save every child from fear and pain. I want to tell people that you can live through a storm of bullets and come out whole. I want kids to stay in school and parents to think about how their actions affect their children. When deciding to publish this book, there was no choice. I feel that my whole life has been about this and future books. I associate every trauma with a chapter. I feel strongly that I had to survive these events in order to help others survive.

It's mostly about survival. Between the bullets, recklessness of my parents, my careless and constant drug use, and the way I would run off with any man who asked—I should have been killed, been permanently damaged, or destined to a life filled with pain and suffering. What I am is grateful—for every moment that I have with my kids, for a sunny day, for the honest way I am able to express myself, and for the people around me who keep me going.

Is Bullets, then, a fairy tale? Not quite. The big bad wolf still finds a way into my house. My memoir did not stop with the death of my dad. Weirdness follows me. This is what I have gotten used to. People tell me I am strong. I think I'm numb from it all. I always have a story. This is my favorite greeting to people. I always ask, "What's your story?" I seldom get one. I figure everyone should have at least one story. For those who don't, I am happy to lend a few of mine.